UNFILTERED

Beneath the noise of our thoughts lies
the true narrative of our minds.
An honest journey into psychology
when the masks finally come off.

Dr. Patricia A. Farrell

author of
How to Be Your Own Therapist

Copyright

ISBN: 979-8-9886544-9-0

BOOKS by Patricia A. Farrell, Ph.D. (may be purchased on a number of platforms, not limited to Amazon)

How to Be Your Own Therapist: A Step-by-Step Guide to Taking Back Your Life

It's Not All in Your Head: Anxiety, Depression, Mood Swings & Multiple Sclerosis

Work Stress: How You Can Beat It

A Social Security Disability Psychological Claims Handbook

A Social Security Disability Psychological Claims Guidebook for Children's Benefits

The Disability Accessible US Parks in All 50 States: A Comprehensive Guide

Birding in the US NOW!: A birding guide for individuals with disabilities

Sleep, Insomnia, Stress:: What you don't know can hurt you

A Mind on Fire: Questioning Madness, Medicine and Life

Fired Up:: A journey through psychiatry, TV and the wonders of life

Flash Fiction

Unexpected Short Tales of Surprise

Contents

UNFILTERED

INTRODUCTION

When I first started writing these articles, I felt I needed to find a way to navigate the vast amount of health information available today. That's my purpose here. All of the articles are intentionally brief, think pieces, and, as is everything that has to do with health or science, all of them will experience updates over time. Keep this in mind because updating your knowledge is important, and no book can ever be current immediately after it's published. The nature of science and medicine is such that it is a continuing process of discovery, and that is where your continuing research must be.

Throughout my career, I have been fortunate to observe how people's attitudes toward mental health have evolved over the years and how it is often easier to believe myths than to distinguish between information and misinformation. Sometimes, the material seems too difficult to understand, but it's always been my belief that, if it is presented in a fashion that is understandable, you should have no problem following it. I base this on personal experience in subjects such as statistics, biology, chemistry, and even computer programming. I never found one book that totally answered the questions or made it easier for me to understand. Often, I had at least five books on any single topic in my personal library. That is a belief that I carry to this day and that I recommend you use in your learning journey. Don't take just one source; look for three or four.

This collection provides you with information that I would offer to a friend or a patient in real life, without the usual marketing and in a format that is easily applicable to daily life. The topics are wide-ranging, you will note, and that also is my purpose because we are curious creatures, and that is one of our strong points. Curiosity, according to the old chestnut, may have "killed the cat," but it is something you should hold precious and maintain no matter what force you may face.

Always be curious and always be asking questions to clarify anything you don't understand. I used to say to my students that I didn't believe there was anything they couldn't understand. If they had a problem understanding, perhaps it was the instructor's difficulty in using appropriate methods to help them see the material and understand it. Even difficult subjects can be brought down to much simpler terms to make them something to be learned, not feared. I'm sorry that so many people often find themselves saying, "Oh, I can't do that." I'm not sure that's true. Some of us do have an easier time digesting specific topics, but it doesn't mean the rest of us can't also be successful students in those areas. **Trust yourself and seek the sources.**

I have been interested in the mind-body paradigm and its unexplained phenomena for a long time. You will notice this as a theme throughout the chapters that include arguments about the effects of microplastics in the environment, how grief actually works (it's not as simple as Kubler-Ross' five stages, by the way), or the importance of good oral care to prevent cancer or heart issues. I have also written about the benefits of dancing, the importance of sleep, and the side effects of not getting enough sleep; the strengths of fermented foods as they relate to health; and the risks of overdependency on technology, including sleep tracking devices, in your everyday life.

I am particularly interested in some of the areas where I think we have gotten it wrong. My piece on medical skepticism and conditions like ME/CFS is based on the observations of the system failing to deliver where it should for the people it is intended to help the most. In the same way, my work on parental stress is inspired by the impact of our mental health on family dynamics.

When it comes to health trends, I try to maintain critical thinking and look for the bright side. Whether discussing the health benefits of fermented foods or the overuse of sleep tracking devices, my goal is to offer clear insights into what is genuine and what is merely marketing, such as the 10K steps. I investigated the issues, and I also looked into the difficulties of raising a child with ADHD while struggling with anxiety and the challenges of stress management in a toxic workplace. Life presents many challenges, and one of the things that we can use to meet those challenges is critical thinking, and that's where I have attempted to raise issues, pro and con, where it is appropriate. Even in research, there are often no definitive answers to questions. Rather, there are areas of gray with much to be explored in the future. In fact, that must be one of the drivers for people to enter research—there is so much to be discovered still.

When so many people are overwhelmed by health information, I wrote this collection to provide some sense of it all in an "unfiltered" way. I didn't want to add one more set of facts to the already overwhelming trove out there. I wanted to provide context to help you understand the role of the mind, the exciting new discoveries between the gut microbiome and the mind, the body, and the environment in your life. These articles are offered as potential conversations, beginnings, if you will, that could have happened between friends if the two had some free time.

In a world where health information is often packaged and presented as simple, straightforward solutions, I decided to be raw and real—to share with you research findings and the many remaining mysteries. I wanted these articles to guide you as you travel through the world of healing and self-discovery. I also wanted to present, where possible, that many of the titans of their fields have feet of clay and some had very difficult personality disorders and major ego problems.

Some individuals hastily formed conclusions based on their personal emotions, instead of conducting thorough research to substantiate their hypotheses. In those instances, a significant number of people hastily believed everything they wrote or said, leaving us with the task of undoing the damage these major myth makers caused. Women, unfortunately, have suffered the most from the lack of their involvement in much of the major research studies. As a result, diagnosis and treatment lagged behind that for men. Even in the area of heart attacks, an area where I am not an expert, the symptoms in a woman are decidedly different from those in a man. Now, researchers are attempting to catch up on this major issue.

Essentially, I aimed to create an opportunity for you, and now it's up to you to choose whether or not to embark on the path I've laid out for you—a decision I believe you'll find appealing. After all, what's at stake here? It's your life, and you want to make it the best you can; do it. Read and begin the path toward improvement and increased knowledge.

<u>One note on this book's cover.</u> Why a dandelion seed ball? It's a metaphor for the content of this book that will, like the tiny wind-blown seeds of this plant, become a tiny information "seed" in your mind that will grow as you add to your knowledge.

Chapter 1: The Myth of the Gospel of 10,000 Steps Daily for Health

Wellness experts are shouting from the rooftops that anyone who wants to maintain their health must, if at all possible, **walk at least 10,000 steps each day.** The idea is a marketing myth, but it has spread like wildfire among the entire wellness community. People who don't adhere to this mandate are made to feel guilty, ashamed, and in need of some strict instruction. But where did this idea germinate? Moreover, why do we believe this so readily without any justification or science behind it? Is it just word-of-mouth and then it becomes "truth?" Whenever we begin to believe anything like this, it's in our best interest to question where it came from and from whom it came. Be your own detective here because it's in your best interest.

In the 1960s, Japan was where the concept of 10,000 steps first emerged. **Manpo-kei, or "10,000 steps meter,"** is the *name of a pedometer* created by the Yamasapedometer firm. The business promoted the idea that getting 10,000 steps a day is essential for good health when marketing this product. Unfortunately, *there isn't enough evidence to support the idea* that everyone should walk 10,000 steps each day to achieve optimal health. The precise number of 10,000 steps was **selected more for its catchy quality** than for its basis in fact. The idea, therefore, wasn't so much that it was a good thing to do for health, but that it was a good match with their marketing program.

More complex understandings of the health advantages of exercise have been gained through scientific studies on physical activity. Adults should engage in at least 150 minutes of moderate-intensity aerobic activity each week, according to the World Health Organization (WHO) and the Centers for Disease Control and Prevention (CDC). This recommendation places *more emphasis on participating in activities* that increase breathing and heart rate than it does on counting steps. We also know that, in addition to being good for our physical health, exercise helps with our mental health. Certainly, walking is one of the easiest exercise exercises for us and anyone has that available to them free of charge.

The 10,000-step goal **does not take into account individual variations in *physical fitness** levels, age, weight, or pre-existing medical conditions.* Are you seeing some problems with this now? When it comes to exercise, every person has different demands. For those with physical limitations or those new to exercise, setting a fixed goal of

10,000 steps per day *may not be appropriate or realistic, and it might have worse consequences.*

Also, studies have revealed that *more importance is placed on the type and intensity of physical exercise* than on merely completing a predetermined number of steps. Compared to low-intensity activities like brisk strolling, high-intensity workouts and exercises that test various muscle groups have been demonstrated to offer greater health advantages. But this type of exercise must be limited to those who have all the physical health prerequisites for it.

You can rest assured that walking is a very effective form of exercise, despite the fact that the **10,000-step rule was a marketing gimmick** with weak scientific support. Instead of being fixated on a precise step count, it's critical to concentrate on personalized fitness goals and engage in activities that suit your unique talents and interests. Consulting with medical experts or fitness experts can help create an activity plan that is unique to your needs and maximizes health benefits.

Chapter 2: Grieve As You Must, and Break Free of Believing in the "Stages"

*Y*ears ago, just after my mother had died in hospice care for her metastatic cancer, a nurse from the unit at the hospital called me. She inquired about my well-being and then expressed shock, annoyance, and a hint of shame (for me) that I hadn't started going through the traditional—and completely incorrect—stages of grieving. The nurse was, in fact, lecturing me as though I were a child, which was quite a long time ago. It was disrespectful. I was fortunate in that, at the time, I was doing book reviews for my job, and a small book on hospice care came over my desk. I read it, and I found information that was useful not only regarding care but also where it could be obtained in the US at that time. I also examined the reported stages of grief, which this nurse wholeheartedly embraced.

I was not only taken aback by that woman's approach to me in my grief; I was angry. Here I was, totally wrecked when my mother died after months of our caring for her at home, and she was lecturing me on how I was doing it all wrong. I will never forget that phone call and cutting her off. After that, I never responded to the few calls that came from the hospice unit in the hospital. I'd had enough shaming from her. The point here, and one I want to make for anyone who is grieving, is that **there is no formula for grieving,** and any health professional who adheres to it has been misled.

Grieving is an unavoidable aspect of being human. When a loved one passes away, a relationship ends, or you lose your job, there is a process that happens after a loss. Many individuals think that to grieve and heal, there are specific actions that must be taken. I and others, however, refute the idea of a predetermined series of stages and encourage readers to abandon this thinking. I'd like to present a different viewpoint on sorrow and inspire people to accept their individual path to recovery.

As Kubler-Ross stated her unscientific method of devising these alleged stages of grief, she explained it this way. "I was to do the interview while they [her students] stood around the bed watching and observing. We would then retire to my office and discuss our reactions and the patient's response. We believed that by doing many interviews like this, we would get a feeling for the terminally ill and their needs, which in turn we were ready to gratify if possible."

The idea of stages of grief, or as Kubler-Ross later called it, stages of loss, relates to her grief surrounding the death of her father and her anger related to it. It's an unrecognized bias on her part. Also, the stages were based on interviews with dying patients (14 in all), not individuals who were experiencing loss. Grief or bereavement fluctuates over time and does not necessarily lead to acceptance. How can anyone possibly use their own subjective feelings obtained by interacting with a small group of people who were dying of cancer and then try to apply it to the entire grieving world? It is an example of hubris gone wild.

What did she say the stages of grief should be? As she outlined, they were **denial, anger, bargaining, depression, and acceptance**. Not everyone will experience grief that way, and some may be longer in their depression than others, while some will come to acceptance sooner.

But scientists have a tendency to put quantifiable numbers on research. It has happened with most research in the early 20th century when psychology was attempting to wrest validity from the "hard" sciences since psychology was considered a "soft" one. Critical reviews have not agreed with Kubler-Ross, and it may not be in such favor among healthcare professionals today.

Grief is a highly individualized experience. Each person's experience of sorrow is unique and influenced by their personality, life experiences, and the particulars of the loss. Realizing that there is no one-size-fits-all method of grieving is crucial. Following an exact set of instructions can be restrictive and may not be consistent with everyone's experiences. It is essential to respect and validate your feelings instead and to let yourself grieve in a way that is true for you.

And grieving is difficult. A wide range of feelings, from sadness and rage to confusion and remorse, describes it. It doesn't follow a straight line with a definite start, middle, and end. With the ebb and flow of deep emotions, grief can be unpredictable. You can give yourself permission to experience all the feelings that come up without condemnation or expectation by accepting the messy nature of grieving. Grieving can be done in any way; there's no right or wrong.

The idea of going through a sequence of stages suggests a straight path to recovery. But sadness doesn't progress in a straight line. It is more like a jumbled web of feelings and encounters. The notion that one must go through particular phases or stages **oversimplifies the complexity of grieving**. It is crucial to recognize that healing is a journey rather than a destination.

Belief in "stages" can also lead to the bereaved person having irrational expectations. If you don't follow the set timeline or experience emotions out of the intended order, it may result in feelings of inadequacy or failure. You can release yourself from these expectations and allow your grieving journey to develop spontaneously and authentically by letting go of the belief in stages.

Lift the curtain of awareness and look at how the idea of these steps for grieving came to be. For one, it is based on extremely limited and flawed research by Dr. Kubler-Ross and her students, who studied a very limited number of grieving people and then replaced their own beliefs on what they felt was happening. What type of research is this? It's not research, but self-reflection that is highly biased and, arguably, lacks any type of research acumen. But because she was a highly respected psychiatrist, the idea of the stages took hold and quickly became the standard for how grief develops over time after a loss. She was, after all, now a best-selling author, and people were offering courses in death and dying or the stages of grief, either in communities or at colleges. The damage was beginning.

The type of loss experienced, the person's support network, and their coping mechanisms all play a role in how long the mourning process lasts from person to person. It's crucial to give the time and room required for healing.

Getting professional assistance, such as therapy or counseling, can be helpful when grieving. A qualified expert can offer assistance, direction, and resources to help people through the difficult feelings and issues that come with grieving.

Talking to a close friend or trusted relative, exercising, using relaxation techniques like deep breathing or meditation, writing, or joining a support group are all good ways to deal with loss.

Even after a long period of time has passed since the loss, **grief might reappear**. Anger-inducing occasions such as anniversaries, holidays, or triggering incidents might do this. Sorrow is not something that has fully passed or been dealt with. Integrating the loss into one's life may take a lifetime. For some, there will always be the element of grief for a loss, and that simply means the love was strong.

Essentially, think of grieving as a difficult journey that cannot be broken down into a series of actions or phases. And there is no shame in not grieving according to any formula for it. As one research paper noted, "If there are no typical responses to loss and no typical losses, and not everyone goes through them or in order, how can there possibly be stages that universally represent people's reactions to loss? The fact is, no study has ever established that stages of grief actually exist, and what are defined as such can't be called stages."

Chapter 3: Simple Touch Mandates a Significant Place in Health Fostering

Once, on a trip with a friend to Mexico, she became ill as we were in a small airport waiting room, seated on benches against the wall. As we sat there, a middle-aged Mexican couple came over to sit beside us, and as they did, the woman began moving closer to my friend. She moved so close that their arms and shoulders were touching, and the two of us, being strangers, wondered if something criminal would happen. Now, we live in a world where concerns about any type of touch, except those from a parent or close relative, might be questioned. For this overzealous and negligent approach, we pay a high price.

In that small airport, I did learn something that, in years to come, would begin a new perspective for me on touch. The man at the airport, sensing our concern, turned and said with a smile, "My wife sees your friend isn't well and is sitting with her to give her strength." I hadn't thought much about it, but recent *research is pointing to the power of human touch* and how it is vital that we incorporate it into not simply our lives **but even our healthcare**. I don't know if there is a psychic component, such as the Mexican woman sitting next to my friend, but that has yet to be explored, and perhaps it will also offer new insights.

The pandemic brought attention to the idea of touch, and now we need a deeper understanding of the ways in which **physical touch** and the absence **of it** when we withdraw socially *can impact our psychological and physical health.*

From aiding development and growth to **buffering against anxiety and stress,** the most common touch interventions—like kangaroo **care for newborns or massage for adults—have** a broad range of mental and physical health benefits that *persist throughout the lifespan* of both animals and humans.

Although there is a great deal of evidence in the literature supporting the benefits of touch, there is also *variation in the studied groups,* the type and *duration of applied touch,* the *measured health outcomes, the type of person* applying the touch (e.g., a partner versus a stranger), and the outcomes, such as a one-time hug versus repeated 60-minute massages.

During the pandemic, people were anxious about breathing and physical touch, which caused them to *withdraw socially* and experience emotional pain. It provided a brilliant illustration of our need for touch. Some people may not get the non-sexual physical touch they need, which is known as **tactile deprivation**.

According to studies, physical touch positively affects health at all life stages, including reducing *anxiety and strengthening emotional bonds.* Isolated people can find comfort in self-care, pets, or soft touch. But as individuals, we still *rely heavily on the desire for physical touch and human connection to thrive.* One graphic illustration that shows how lack of human touch is important for the maintenance of life and development in infants was the research of **Rene Spitz after World War II** in orphanages. Researchers were startled by the results.

The children were provided with everything that they needed in terms of food, **clothing, and medical care**, but the one thing that was **not provided was human touch**. The result was that the children developed poorly and failed to thrive (aka hospitalism and anaclitic depression), and some died within their first three years or even sooner.

Another important series of research experiments was carried out by Harry Harlow with rhesus monkeys and lack of attachment for infant monkeys. Considered both controversial and inhumane, it nevertheless supported the idea of **tactile comfort** being necessary for the young.

No one has to tell animals about the need for touch, and you can readily see it if you watch kittens together who were sleeping or, as I've recently seen on the Internet, dogs and cats slumbering together. I've even seen a hen that had been used to hatch duck eggs lovingly care for her ducks and try to cover them beneath her at night as they all slept. It was genuinely touching.

One Touch Impediment

Unfortunately, the pandemic and other easily spread diseases have made people less likely *to connect with each other in person.* Not only are handshakes not accepted anymore, but other forms of touch may not be enough to have the same positive effect. Because of this, our society has been affected by our need to be careful about touching, closeness, and physical interactions.

We must wonder if a caring or interested look can make up for the fact that we cannot touch as before. Is there another way to achieve the same kind of biological process that has an impact on our mental and physical health? Future study is the only way to find out what factors were at play and how to move forward.

Touch treatments are suitable for your mental and physical health. And touch interventions have been shown to help *reduce depression and worry in adults, children, and newborns*. They can also *help newborns gain weight*. These results agree with those of earlier research on this subject.

Researchers found that more touch sessions correlated with better results, such as *pain in adults*. Chronic illnesses that make people depressed and anxious often happen at the same time as loneliness. It is possible to ameliorate this through touch. Knowing the toucher did not change the health benefits for either adults or children. On the other hand, newborns' general health benefits were affected by familiarity, with a touch from a parent being better than a touch from medical staff.

One more thing about touch that study papers talk about shows how important it is for *kids' intellectual growth*. Students who had their teachers gently touch them seemed to do better in school than students who did not get this kind of physical support. But, in a world concerned about inappropriate touch, it can be assumed that teachers and other mentors of children would be more unwilling to engage in any type of touch.

Overall, how can we suitably engage in touch? It's still an issue to be resolved in a culture that has recognized so much inappropriate touching, that true empathic touch is often denied. Touch remains one of our most basic and primitive forms of *attachment, belonging, and safety*. It also engages specific, healthy hormone production, as well as helping to maintain our immune system. Therefore, **touch cannot be dismissed** since it is a potent form of health maintenance.

Chapter 4: Anxiety Begone: Slaying Your Dragon to Free Yourself for Public Speaking

P ublic speaking anxiety, also known as glossophobia, is one of the world's most common phobias, which affects 75% of people globally and even **surpasses the fear of death** in some cases. It is a widespread issue that cuts across cultural, socio-economic, and professional life, affecting everyone from students to chief executives. No one chief executive had such difficulty separating his performance anxiety that he joined a specific group to learn how to make presentations and handle his anxiety effectively. A group did prove to be beneficial, and he went on to form his own company and make presentations worldwide.

The NIMH points out that specific anxiety about public speaking can adversely impact *career, academic, and personality growth*. However, many people don't know that such an anxiety response can be redefined and even utilized as *a valuable resource* for performance enhancement. The physical feelings that people get when they speak in front of a crowd, such as increased heart rate, increased alertness, and a surge of adrenaline, are the same as those that help athletes perform at their best.

First, it is crucial to *know the causes of speaking anxiety* to manage it properly. Some common anxiety triggers include *fear of being judged, past experiences, lack of readiness, and high standards*. This knowledge alone can help make speakers less nervous, allowing the audience to perceive them as 50 times more confident than they are.

Several evidence-based strategies effectively manage presentation anxiety. One helps relieve physical and mental stress by **contracting and relaxing all the muscles** in the body. We can do this in a few minutes before speaking, and it has been proven to ease anxiety symptoms by 60% in some cases.

Another effective strategy, **cognitive restructuring**, involves **changing negative cognitive distortions**. For instance, instead of saying, "*I am going to make a mistake*," presenters can say, "*This is my chance to convey my information*." Cognitive restructuring can help reduce public speaking anxiety by 75% if done consistently.

I recall having a student call me from his medical school on his first night there. Once he arrived at the school, he was quickly surrounded by students there who began to tell him that he should leave and not remain. The other students were so anxious and upset; they upset him too and made him feel that he should leave. When I heard this, I immediately realized that he, being an incredibly gifted, science-oriented student, would present a possible threat to the other students grades. He was going to make it much harder for the professors to write on a curve, which the students had become accustomed to in previous semesters.

I didn't agree with him leaving and told him to have dinner with the dean that evening, if at all possible. He stayed, graduated at the top of his class, and is now a medical director for a nationwide service. He conquered his public speaking anxiety when he had that initial dinner and interacted with students the next day. Presentations were never a problem from that point on.

An additional way to slay this dragon depends on **preparation and practice**, as these remain the fundamental factors. The step-by-step process of the "3P" model. What is it? The current communication research supports **preparation, practice, and presentation**. Under thorough preparation, consider the following: the content to *be delivered, the target audience, what to do during delivery, and the environment* where the speech is to be given are all known. Research also shows that presenters who have rehearsed their presentation **three or more times outperform** and have less anxiety than those who have not.

Another aspect of speaking anxiety that needs attention is **physical preparation,** although most people don't know this. *Our body language plays a significant role in how we feel about ourselves.* It makes us more confident and less anxious, especially when using **power poses** for two minutes before speaking, as this lowers cortisol and increases testosterone.

Breathing control is another highly recommended strategy; the 4–7–8 method (take in a breath for four seconds, hold it for seven seconds, and exhale for eight seconds) helps to regulate the nervous system and reduce anxiety symptoms.

The good news is that *some level of anxiety may be helpful*. The issue is to find a way to utilize this energy. One study showed that perceiving anxiety as excitement can enhance performance. You can change the nervous energy into a positive and energetic delivery by telling yourself, "I am excited," instead of trying to calm down.

Strategies

Some of the strategies that can be used here are:

1. Get there early enough to get acquainted with the environment and check the equipment

2. Begin with a pleasant, welcoming message you have memorized

3. Concentrate on the message you are conveying rather than on your performance

4. Use movement and gestures so that the nervousness can be used effectively

5. Using pauses enables you to gather your thoughts and control the rate of delivery

6. Make sure there is water nearby and take brief breaks when necessary

The short-term advantages of managing and reducing speaking anxiety are significant, but the long-term advantages are even greater. Overcoming public speaking fears leads to **career satisfaction, faster promotions, and more leadership roles.**

Effective public speakers earn 10% more than their peers with similar qualifications but without the latter's public speaking skills. But there's one more technique that can be highly effective, and that is *how you physically present yourself.*

Use Power Poses

What are some examples of "power poses"? Power poses are *expansive body postures* that can increase feelings of confidence and power while decreasing feelings of stress. Here are some specific examples:

1. The Wonder Woman/Superman Pose

a. Stand with feet shoulder-width apart, hands firmly on hips.

b. Chest lifted, shoulders back

c. Head held high

d. Hold for 2–3 minutes. This is one of the most researched and effective power poses.

2. The Victory Pose

a. Stand tall with arms raised in a "V" shape above head

b. Chin lifted

c. Chest expanded

d. Feet slightly apart

e. Such as what athletes do after winning

3. The Presenter Stance

a. Standing straight

b. Arms spread wide, taking up space

c. Palms facing up or forward

d. Feet planted firmly about shoulder-width apart

The confidence gained from overcoming public speaking can be applied to other aspects of life. People who overcome speaking anxiety have mentioned that they *enjoy better relations with other people, solve problems better, and are more steadfast in the face of other challenges.* Preparing for speaking anxiety also helps develop skills that apply to other aspects of life, such as preparation, focus, and emotional control.

It's not about being 100 percent comfortable, but rather learning to be comfortable with being uncomfortable. Each time anyone participates in a speaking activity, they can try out these strategies and build on their confidence. It's important not to try to eradicate anxiety but to find a way to work with it to become a positive factor in performance and self-development.

Chapter Five

Chapter 5: Beware the "Evil" Therapist

A therapist or, more appropriately, a psychotherapist, in this case, is a word we never associate with evil. The word evil is reserved for use in the religious realm, as is the concept of the Devil (see Elaine Pagels' "The Origin of Satan" or Bart Ehrman's "God's Problem").

With the popularization of therapy, possibly related to its extolling by the wealthy and famous and the availability of health insurance, change has come. Psychiatrists even considered whether or not "evil" exists in anyone. Were there evil people (like Jeffrey Dahmer, John Wayne Gacy, and Dennis Rader) or were they exhibiting a form of mental illness or a personality disorder?

The question now has theoretical consideration as well as medical and legal implications. Does evil exist, or are we reverting to a less enlightened age where religion explained all for us in our wish to have answers?

Psychotherapy is dependent on introspection, but if evil exists in some persons, is this concept relevant? An evil drive pushing toward acts concomitant with it wouldn't seem open to change by careful inspection of one's psyche. If someone with a predilection toward skirting the rules of ethics related to psychotherapy were to be in a position of power, what would they do? Could they harm us in some way? If so, what would the harm be?

We need only read some of the newspaper reports of questionable or unethical behavior of famous therapists such as Freud. What did Freud do? For one thing, he pressured patients to contribute to his therapy association. That is unethical. Then, too, Freud considered his patients "riff-raff" and convinced one man that he was a homosexual, urged him to divorce his wife, and marry another of his patients.

Urging his patients to rid themselves of their neuroses, Freud failed to heal himself from the serious anxiety that stopped him from facing his patients (he sat in a chair at the head of his famous couch) and his enuresis. And let's not forget his addiction to small, black cigars, which he smoked repeatedly all day long. A neurosis, perhaps? Read Jeffrey Masson's book, "The Assault on Truth: Freud's Suppression of the Seduction Theory." And be sure to read "Freud and His Followers" because it reveals the man, not the demi-god we've been led to believe he was. Freud was petty, vain, and unforgiving when someone in his circle refused to accept his interpretation of things. For that reason, when Carl Jung questioned him, he responded by demoting Jung (Freud's intended heir apparent) in his professional circle in Austria and would even cross the street rather than wish him a good day if he saw him outdoors. He never forgave Jung.

An additional case of severe concern to all of us is the one where one of Freud's female patients almost bled to death. He believed that a nerve in the nose was causing her to engage in excessive sexual self-stimulation, and he had an associate operate on her nose. The surgery was a failure. The patient, Emma Eckstein, nearly died following the surgery. Although Eckstein suffered irreversible facial disfigurement, she went on to become a psychoanalyst. Of course, this is an example of not only extreme hubris, but a lack of understanding of biology.

One area where we can find a specific instance of Freud falling victim to his own theorizing is in the case of "Little Hans." The child had a terrible fear of horses, and Freud diagnosed this as a fear of his father castrating him because his father was so powerful. This "castration complex" was actually a phobia that the boy had developed after a serious carriage accident with a horse that resulted in his fear, not of his father castrating him.

Women who came to Freud with a specific "neurosis" were likewise seen as suffering from unacceptable sexual impulses toward their fathers. In his Victorian world, Freud refused to believe that these women had been victims of sexual assault by their fathers, and he turned it around to the women being neurotic. This was one of the things that Masson noted in his book regarding the seduction theory.

What about the equally famous Albert Ellis, the father of Rational Emotive Behavioral Therapy, who was not the monogamous type? He admitted to having sex with patients, though only after treatment had ended. In some states that might be acceptable, but not everywhere. In fact, professional acquaintances of mine, who had gone to open seminars with Ellis, noted that he denigrated anyone who came to him and believed that this was perfectly fine. When is it ever "perfectly fine" to make someone who comes for help feel worse because of the way you, as a therapist, treat them? The answer is self-evident; it's never acceptable.

Depending on state licensing laws, therapists may have a relationship with a former patient under certain circumstances. Some states say this is never condoned; others say it's fine two years after therapy has ended. All licensing authorities, too, have a code of ethics by which licensees must abide. But are all therapists licensed, and for what and by whom? These are important questions to ask and to have answered. I knew of a social worker who attempted to deceive his patients into thinking he was a licensed psychologist. How did he do it? First, he called himself "Dr." and had a sign outside his office with that title. Second, his letterhead carried a number under his name that most might think was a license number—it wasn't. It was his business tax number for the state in which he practiced.

Anyone engaged in the mental health field as psychiatrists, psychologists, social workers, or counselors of any stripe needs to be truthful to themselves and their patients. But there are those who are in the field for reasons that, if revealed, would lead to professional sanctions.

Famous or Infamous?

The question of evil in a psychiatric setting would seem to have been settled by an editorial in one of the psychiatry journals.

As one editorial indicated, "*Psychiatrists are medically trained in the scientific method, not in the diagnosis and treatment of evil…. (This) is the province of the philosopher and theologian and… Introducing the concept of evil into forensic psychiatry hopelessly complicates an already difficult task.*"

The editorial writer indicated that evil is an exclusively human quality, and one not observed in animals. He was attempting to address one psychiatrist's formulation of a "Depravity Scale," which was to standardize measures of evil to provide some guidance for other psychiatrists. People love scales, and medical professionals are no different.

In the context of this article, I am not attempting to categorize evil as anything other than a therapist's wishes to optimize power, prestige, individual desires, or money. I do not believe they are genuinely evil, but some are not what I would see as sterling characters. Most try their utmost to deserve the trust their clients place in them. But there are others who, realizing that their patients wish to please them, will take advantage.

I recall an older therapist who was brought up on charges before the licensing board, who had borrowed in excess of $50,000 from one of his patients and had not repaid it at that point. The patient, after attempting several times to recoup his money, reported the therapist to the licensing board. The board, after careful consideration, suspended the man's license and indicated that all current patients had to be referred out to other therapists. His attorney wanted the board to allow him to continue practicing for another year. The board did not agree.

However, some of the most famous names in mental health have been accused of or have committed the most egregious actions. For some, it was a casual concern with their academic preparation (Erik Erickson and Fritz Perls); for others, it is ethical violations, sexual deviancy, murder case involvement, or drug use. Some engaged in unethical research. All of them are human with feet of clay. There is also an ongoing dialogue about whether or not Fritz Perls ever got a medical degree as he claimed.

The media is rife with the more sensational stories of therapists who have engaged in non-professional behavior. For example, they have slept with their patients, borrowed money, been involved in business relationships, controlled their patients' lives as in the case of one famous music star, and generally allowed themselves to freewheel their lives as they wished. Of course, none of this is acceptable and violates ethical guidelines for all of the mental health professions.

Psychotherapists are supposed to help us deal with the difficulties in our lives, but that's not always the case. Too many therapists are unqualified to practice as they do, are not licensed, got degrees from unaccredited schools, lack the training required, or are in it for the money.

Freud detailed his own love of money in his letters, where he referred to it as "laughing gas." Others may have more nefarious reasons for hanging out their shingle. One student at a seminar freely offered to me, "I want to make money!"

According to Dr. Jeffrey Masson, Freud denied the sexual abuse of children. *"The silence demanded of the child by the person who violated her (or him) is perpetuated and enforced by the very person to whom she has come for help,"*

The shingle designating a professional may also be deceptive as it indicates the person is "Doctor..." Does that mean MD, Ph.D., or what? And what type of Ph.D. did they receive? Honesty in this profession, as in others, is not a strong suit for all. How do you tell who to avoid? No one provides guidelines.

<u>The Knaves With Degrees</u>

Plaques on office walls are nothing more than glitzy ads that are supposed to convince you they are qualified in their field; they can buy plenty of them. Brass plaques on office doors also mean nothing. I knew of one therapist who had seven different plaques on the door, each indicating certification in some area of therapy. She was terribly remiss in any knowledge of pharmacology and the dangers of mixing alcohol with specific types of anxiety related medications.

Some therapists are so taken with their alleged ability to perform "semi-miracles" in their patients' lives that they have stated things that are more than unacceptable. For example, one therapist who, in violation of ethics, encouraged group members to socialize and date. I know of this, having heard it from others.

This licensed individual also told one of the patients that if she discontinued therapy with her, the patient would commit suicide within one year. The patient went on to work with another therapist. In a few years, the patient earned her master's degree and then went on to study for a doctorate in psychology. Thoughts of suicide never entered her mind. The therapist remained in practice, and, seemingly, no charges were filed. The patient wanted to walk away and forget about it entirely.

A psychologist, who had a young man referred to her, began to engage in what she called therapeutic sex with the young man. The sessions went on for almost a year. After each sexual encounter in her office, he gave her a check for $150 and scheduled their next session. One of my professors told our class, "*I have never heard of a therapeutic erection,*" when he heard about this. Unfortunately, later, I found out my professor was practicing without a license.

The unethical behavior between the therapist and the young man continued until he worked up the courage to discuss it with his parents. They reported the woman to her licensing board, and the board suspended her license. One of the problems with suspension is that these individuals often return to practice in the future. During the period of supervision, they do nothing untoward, but afterward, we have to wonder. The system, in general, relies on the patient pool and the public to report.

Active violators of ethics or who engage in illegal activities are not sought out by investigators because there are so few who are hired to perform this work. Many states have only two people to look at all the licensed persons within that state. This ongoing surveillance does not include those in the medical profession since they perform their own investigations, but, here too, it is left to someone to report. Often these persons are not reported for a variety of reasons, which may include intimidation, blackmail, or threats of being cut off from treatment or being sued.

But there are things that you can do to clarify any questions you may have about entering therapy, with whom and what you can expect.

<u>Steps to Protect Yourself</u>

A short guide to assist in therapist selection is needed. Here is a list of suggested questions to ask and places to find help should you need it.

1. Do not depend on ads for therapists. Big ads mean that a person is willing to pay for these displays; they are not an indication of anything other than the person's wish to be noticed and to believe that the larger the ad, the more credibility will be associated with that therapist. They will expect to recoup the funds in therapy fees. Ads are no assurance of anything.

2. No one can guarantee you anything. It is against ethical guidelines for psychologists to provide any assurance of results or a guarantee. I heard of one woman who was the chief of psychology at her institution, who took out ads in local newspapers that indicated she guaranteed that her treatment was effective. This was wholly unwarranted and absolutely unethical. One note here, also. A very famous psychiatrist once told me that being the chair of a department in a hospital meant little to him other than that they were adept at hospital politics. This may or may not be true, but he definitely believed it.

3. Ask all the questions where you need answers. Don't permit anyone to intimidate you. You are paying for a service, and you are a customer no matter whether they call you a patient or a client.

4. Some questions: What degree do they have, and in what discipline? A school administration doctorate is not a doctorate in psychology. A doctorate or a Ph.D. needs explanation. Do not skip over this one. Where did they go to school, and where did they do their internship or residency? Plaques on the wall are meaningless. Too many wall decorations can be bought.

I knew of one "therapist" who had a doctorate in school administration but called herself "doctor" everywhere and professed to be a therapist. And, please, take advantage of the search feature on the Internet. Search for anyone's name and all the information that you can find about them. Patient reviews are questionable since not everyone will leave a good review, and some people will leave bad reviews out of spite.

5. What license do they have? Being "certified" is not equivalent to being licensed. Look their license up on the state's licensing board for that specific specialty. You will also be able to see if there have been any malpractice lawsuits filed against them. I know that the state of California regularly issues lists of people who have either had their licenses revoked or suspended and the reasons this has been done. Many times it is for illegal business practices, sometimes for substance abuse.

6. What is their theoretical orientation? Have them explain it to you. Take notes. Google anything you don't understand if they tell you something unusual.

7. What is the treatment plan, and what is the timeframe for your therapy?

8. In what do they specialize? Examples: medical illness, anxiety, stress reduction, family therapy, cognitive-behavioral techniques, etc. Is this person a specialist or someone who treats anyone who comes through the door? No, they're not. We are not dealing with a Chinese restaurant menu here.

9. To which professional organizations do they belong? Google that one, too.

10. What is their cancellation policy? *Insurance cannot be billed for missed sessions.* If they do bill for these sessions, it is insurance fraud.

11. Check online with their licensing board to see if there are any actions pending currently or past violations. Also, check for lawsuits online.

If you need more assistance in deciding whether to report a therapeutic transgression has occurred, where do you go? The usual course would be to your state's licensing board.

An internet search for "(state) licensing board for (psychologists, psychiatrists, social workers, counselors)" should return the result you seek. At this time, there is no national licensing board for the professions.

<u>AI Is Getting in on the Act</u>

As in so many things, technology is being brought into the realm of therapy, but is it free of the problems we've seen in artificial intelligence (AI)? Large data sets are not devoid of major issues of bias, miscalculation, and assumptions.

The construction of an AI algorithm that would help to select a suitable candidate as your therapist remains problematic. Some data sets are heavily loaded in terms of bias. Hidden bias includes ageism, sexism, and racism. Consider how algorithms are formulated. All of them depend on prior bits of computer code that then are incorporated into the algorithm. Once that happens, it is extremely difficult to find the place where the bias entered because the algorithm probably has multiple bits that have been inserted into it. This presents a major issue for anyone working in computers and, especially, in mental health programs that depend on artificial intelligence.

For individuals with specific wishes, such as someone of a similar ethnic background or religion or any other particular, the program may select only those individuals. At the same time, it will exclude individuals who might be better suited in terms of forming a therapeutic relationship.

The Therapeutic Relationship

The therapeutic relationship is the basis of all successful therapies. It is here that you must be most attuned to how you feel when you are in the company of that person. Of course, this assumes that you will have a screening or initial consult after you have selected a therapist.

Would selecting a therapist based on shared demographic features result in a good match? The belief may be that this individual has shared life experiences, which would make them more apt to understand the individual's life experiences. Often, a person who seeks a therapist with a similar racial or ethnic background as a preferred provider may delay therapy while waiting for a "match." But an analysis that looked at individuals matched in terms of background and those who weren't matched indicated the treatment outcomes were similar. Therefore, the therapist doesn't have to share a collective life experience, ethnicity, or other background feature. But AI might skew the results in that direction.

The selection of a therapist is of utmost importance because they are dealing with your life and assisting you to make needed changes. As you would with any significant decision, check carefully, be satisfied, and never hesitate to question. It is your life.

Chapter 6: Can Plastic Damage Your Brain, Your Health, and Your Heart?

*W*ishing to save time and still have a delicious meal has resulted in the growth of new industries providing *pre-made meals in convenient plastic dishes* for microwaving. Could this present any danger to your health? Sure, you will dispose of the plastic dish in a recycling bag and feel everything is fine. But it's not.

What could go wrong? How about the danger to your health from that food, or the dish you heat in that microwave? Cou that present danger to your health? It all comes down to one word—plastics.

Worldwide culture never expected that plastic's fantastic break-through chemistry discovery could endanger humans and the environment. In fact, after World War II and into the 1940s, 50s, and 60s, when plastics emerged along with frozen foods, convenience was **the watchword,** and words like *ecology and environmental sensitivity* had not entered our vocabulary.

We were naïve and wide-eyed at the prospect of what plastics could do for us regarding clothing, household items, construction, automobiles, and anything you could name. Wherever there was a product to be made, plastics could play a role because they were innovative, cheap, and readily available. Plastics built fortunes, and now we see the dark downside of their impact on the world and **our health**.

And it's not just plastics as we see them, but the form of plastic once they break down, known as micro or nanoplastics, that presents a highly disturbing attack on human health. *Trash, dust, textiles, cosmetics, cleaning supplies, rain, seafood, produce, table salt,* and many other sources are where we can find plastic bits. Is sea salt free of this microplastic? No safety there because **the oceans are full of micro- and nanoplastics**.

And we've been absorbing all these various forms of plastic from our environment **for decades**. Scientists in human research have found microplastics in several bodily fluids, including the *placenta, blood, saliva, liver, and kidneys*. Researchers are trying to determine how these *plastics spread to other organs and tissues from the lungs and the gastrointestinal tract*. Because of its ability to penetrate cells, researchers are most concerned about **microplastics smaller than 1 millimeter,** the nanoplastics. These are the truly dangerous forms of plastic found **resident in our brains**.

Plastics in Our Brains

Scientists have found microplastics in human brains at levels far greater than in other organs. The buildup of plastic seems to **be increasing** with time, having **accelerated by 50%** in the last eight years alone. How did it get there, and what is the danger that it presents?

Researchers stress that particular long-term impacts are still unknown, but new evidence suggests that microplastic buildup in human brains is a major health risk. The most concerning conclusion of the study is that microplastic buildup in brain tissue samples has increased at a **rate similar to that of environmental plastic pollution**, with levels higher than in 2016 samples.

Findings of significantly increased amounts of these particles in **brain samples from dementia patients**, particularly around immune cells and along the walls of blood vessels, were a significant cause for concern. Scientists quickly note that *just because there is a correlation does not mean microplastics cause dementia.* The increased concentrations could be caused by changes in brain function caused by dementia, such as a diminished ability to guard the blood-brain barrier.

Potential contributions to *neurological illnesses* and interference with normal brain function are questions where we need answers. The rising presence of microplastics necessitates research on their brain entry, removal, and neurological effects. There is an immediate need for additional research into the long-term impacts of microplastics on human health, and although this study does not establish that microplastics cause specific health problems, it does raise serious concerns about their possible impact on brain function.

Our hearts are incredible pumps that last a lifetime, and even though they are pumping at a rapid rate, micro plastic bits can still be found in it, and it is reason for us to be concerned about our environment.

What About Our Hearts?

Researchers have now shown that microplastics in plaque that blocks arteries in the neck significantly increase **the risk of cardiovascular events like heart attacks and strokes** compared to plaque that does not include plastic.

In a study involving 257 individuals, researchers discovered that **58% of the plaque samples included trace amounts of plastic**, specifically polyethylene and polyvinyl chloride. Those whose plaque contained microplastics had a **mortality, stroke, or heart attack rate that was 4.5 times** greater than that of those whose plaque did not contain microplastics after nearly three years. But, the researchers conclude, they could not state that microplastics were the sole cause of this disturbing statistic, and other factors might be at play here.

Could another factor be the common one-use plastic containers for food that are endemic in our culture? Another study took on this task, and the results were not surprising. In the study, reusable food pouches and plastic containers were tested for the release of microplastics and nanoplastics *under various usage situations*. Results showed that compared to other use scenarios like refrigeration or room-temperature storage, **microwave heating resulted in the largest release of microplastics and nanoplastics into food**. Over the course of three minutes, microwave heating a single square centimeter of plastic in certain containers *released 4.22 million microplastic* and 2.11 billion nanoplastic particles.

However, because it releases the two forms of plastics, that does not resolve the question of how this plastic gets into the organs of our body and, particularly, our brains. It may be involved in our ingesting the plastic, but what happens from there?

Who Is at Greatest Risk

Young people may be more vulnerable because their organs are still maturing. Thyroid cancer is on the rise, and pediatric otolaryngologist and head and neck surgeon Kara Meister, MD, of Stanford Medicine, has seen a correlation between the condition and autoimmune disorders in her patient population. She chose to investigate microplastics because she wanted to know **what could be affecting children's hormones.** There's still much work to be done here and we don't have the answers yet.

How long microplastics remain in the body and how environmental and genetic factors mitigate their effects are yet unknown to scientists. No one has yet decided whether certain polymers or exposure methods are more harmful. We have also not adequately investigated the specific risks microplastics pose to humans. Plastic is so pervasive that strong causal evidence is difficult to come by.

What Can We Do?

Opt for natural fiber clothing, avoid plastic kitchenware, and search for plastic-free cosmetics and toiletries. Prepare your own meals at home and use glass jars for peanut butter and drinks. If you are dining out, bring a glass container. Purchase toys made of metal or wood, and instead of plastic wrap, use foil.

Avoid using plastic containers to reheat food in the microwave. Avoid reusing plastics that have deteriorated because doing so could increase your exposure to particles caused by wear and tear.

There are things we can do to protect ourselves from this day forward, but we will have already ingested and implanted in our organs microplastics from prior years. **Does this mean we should give up trying to avoid plastic?** No, it means that we need to change our lifestyle and purchase choices as well as how we prepare or reheat foods at home.

Is all of this worth it? Ask yourself whether your health has any value to you or how valuable your children's health is to you. Once you've answered those two questions, you will know how to proceed in the future.

Chapter 7: Will You Live to Be 100, and What Safeguards Do You Need to Preserve Your Body and Mind?

Living beyond 70 or even 80 isn't unusual these days, but there are reasons some people live longer, and you need to do a few things. A woman in Spain recently lived to age 117. Once they examined her body, they found that her gut *microbiome was that of an infant,* and she had some type of genetic variant. She died in August 2025.

Are you prepared to live to be 100 or older, and if that should happen, are you planning for it? Some would say it's a dream, and others see it as a financial or medical impossibility. But **we have some control over aging, and it**'s not too late to start planning now. In fact, we have a little-known word for those between 90–99 now, and it's **nonagenarian**.

Have you noticed how many famous entertainers in film and music are living over the age of 80? Here's a short list of some of them:

Dick Van Dyke — 99

Tom Selleck—80

Willie Nelson—91

Jane Fonda — 87

Deborah Harry — 80

Mick Jagger — 81

Tom Jones — 84

Al Pacino—84

Carol Burnett—91

Jack Nicholson—87

Eva Marie Saint—100

Francis Ford Coppola—85

The list is quite impressive, and we might say these individuals are living longer because they have access to excellent healthcare. But they also have the ability to maintain *lifestyles* that allow them to engage in *exercise, meaningful work, and involvement in learning* new career activities.

The famous "Nun Study" of older nuns in an American Midwest convent showed that both earlier education *and learning new challenging activities* benefit cognitive and physical health. More than one nun has lived over the age of 100, and the oldest was 105 and still cognitively intact when she died. In fact, each day she knitted a pair of booties for babies in a local hospital.

Several of the nuns have set themselves a yearly task for learning. One learns a new language each year, and another tries a new skill of any type. Each step to learning provides nourishment for nerve growth in the brain and can reinvigorate nerve cells that may have lost something in their lack of reinforcement by disuse.

The original study's work and its insights resulted in a book, "Aging with Grace." All of this means that those in entertainment and religious activities have something psychologists call "a sense of purpose." But it's not limited to them. I've written about this sense of purpose on Medium.com, and you can pull that up if you would like to read it.

According to the United Nations, about 722,000 individuals were 100 years old or older in 2024. Compared to the projected number of centenarians in 2020, this is a rise, and advances in medicine and artificial intelligence may push that number even higher.

With an estimated 108,000, slightly higher than the Census Bureau's estimate, the United *States of America has the world's second-largest* centenarian population. Japan has the highest population of 100-plus-year-olds (146,000). The top five are completed by Thailand (38,000), India (48,000), and China (60,000).

Less than one percent of the total population in each of these nations is 100 years old or older, yet when added together, they constitute over half (55%) of the global total. People are mainly concerned about their physical health when discussing longevity. However, there are other factors. There is now an unacceptable disparity between health and average longevity. We now have a higher probability of living than remaining healthy for a specific amount of time. If we want to reap the benefits of longer lives, we must narrow this disparity.

That being said, you are capable of a great deal. Our actions and *surroundings* determine the *rate of aging by about 80%.* No amount of advertising can replace a *healthy diet, enough sleep, regular exercise, and listening to your doctor* when they tell you what to do. Even while that advice is getting a scientific upgrade, the important change is that you now have the expectation of becoming older (the old-old as it's known), which is a strong incentive to follow it.

Stem Cells May Be One Key

Research over the previous decades has discovered depositories of what are known as pluripotent stem cells that can be encouraged to become whatever cells we need. The discovery of this type of cell in centurions has sparked new research into harvesting and managing these cells in *treatments for neurodegenerative disorders.*

While most of us may be familiar with the term stem cell, we have generally been taught to believe that most of ours were used during our body's development, but there are reservoirs in specific areas of our body. We know that an area just above the roof of the mouth and the bottom of the brain is rich in these cells that could be harvested to *treat a patient with their own biological material.* These cells have incredible potential.

Neural stem cells have an eternal home in the brain's hippocampus and are capable of differentiating into neurons and glial cells. We are now on the horizon of what is known as regenerative medicine, which is still in its infancy.

It's unclear whether the cataloging of all the areas of stem cells has been achieved, and there may yet be new ones to be discovered. Are stem cells the answer to positive hyper-aging? Perhaps they might be, but does that mean that only those with a specific type of stem cell will live to be 100 years old? That would mean that the rest of us who do not have this genetic predisposition must turn to other forms of life enhancement as we wait for medical advances. Where might those opportunities for increased age maintenance be?

<u>DIY Life Lengthening</u>

Artificial intelligence may speed up scientific breakthroughs in longevity and stem cell use, but while we wait, there are things we can do now that are under our control. What are several things we may begin to utilize now? Here is a selection for your choice and your inclusion in your life.

Tips for a healthy lifestyle in 2025 that promote positive aging include getting plenty of exercise, eating a plant-based diet, not smoking, getting a good night's sleep, dealing with stress, making friends, challenging yourself intellectually, finding meaning in life, and having an optimistic outlook on getting older.

One additional point needs to be made here, and that is specifically about diet, whether non-vegetarian or meat-based or even plant-based or vegan. It has to do with what you do after you have taken any antibiotics for an illness.

Antibiotics kill the good bacteria in your gut, and these are the very ones that are going to protect you from disease. *You need to replenish them* by either eating things like kimchi, pickles, sauerkraut, and, of course, yogurt with active cultures. The bacteria are not replenished immediately, and it may take a week or two. Please do your own research on how long you would need to engage in diet change in this immune-protection area.

When you consider exercise, don't think of it as merely a way to maintain your balance, *your strength, and your ability to move easily.* Exercise has been found to have an important input in your body's release of mood-enhancing hormones and maintaining neural connections. *It doesn't matter what type of exercise you choose*, as long as you do it perhaps three times a week, if that's possible, or once a week.

Get little 1-pound dumbbells, sit in a chair, and do arm exercises for 5 to 10minutes. That's fine. You can find simple exercises for all ages on YouTube.

I always recommend that people go to YouTube with two guys who are rehab specialists. Bob and Brad will give you all the simple exercises that you need and that you can do with *little to no equipment in your home.* A large can of tomatoes can serve as a weight for tricep development. Look it up. No need to go to the gym or pay any fees for a trainer. Look at their videos.

Work up to whatever makes you comfortable, and don't think what someone else does is appropriate for you. *Everybody's body makeup is individual,* and it will let you know when you are pushing it too far or too hard. *Never exercise to the point of pain* because that means you've done too much and could cause damage. Enthusiasm is fine, but curb it. Start slowly and maintain your pace. *This race is one for the tortoise, not the hare.*

Social connections are also highly important, and during these interactions, laugh as much as possible. Believe it or not, laughing is a great exercise and a mood elevator. I've seen it suggested by some therapists that people have a small book with a joke of the day that will make them laugh. Great advice.

One exercise routine that is very much intended for older adults includes tai chi, a wonderful form of slow-motion moves that allows you to gradually achieve more physical stability. In the process, it also encourages mindfulness that relieves stress. We know that relieving stress *helps your immune system*—you can ward off illnesses with a healthy immune system working for you. Remember those centenarians? They were able to make it through the COVID-19 epidemic and other illnesses because they had healthier immune systems.

Considering everything, we do have a great deal at our disposal, even if we don't have those special stem cells that the centenarians seem to possess. Work with what you have, and you can be healthier and happier and maintain your cognition in the process.

Chapter Eight

Chapter 8: Autism May Begin in the Gut, and Antibiotics Could Be Involved

Individuals who have been diagnosed with anything on the autism spectrum have been the object of both ridicule and enthrallment, the breadth of which is astounding to everyone, including those with this diagnosis. Only in the past few decades have we come to see the diagnosis as multifactorial, including both those who have problematic social skills as well as those who can view the world in new, creative ways.

Some of these individuals have achieved extraordinary roles in our culture and climbed to the highest heights regarding creativity and management responsibilities. Therefore, we need to *respect everyone with a diagnosis of autism as an individual* and not simply a diagnosis.

Although there is **no single cause or pathophysiology for autism**, present diagnostic criteria are associated with around *200 hereditary and environmental factors*. Hundreds of different patterns of restricted and *repetitive interests and activities*, as well as persistent difficulties in *social communication and interaction*, are permissible under the current DSM-5 criteria for an autism spectrum disorder (ASD). This broad phenotypic variation has caused **numerous researchers to doubt the ASD diagnosis**, and it seems to have grown significantly in the past two decades.

Autism Myths Exposed as Damaging to Individuals

The spread of false information must be countered with what we currently know from verifiable research. Knowing what is true and what is false can greatly improve your experience if you are autistic, a parent of an autistic child, or both. Here are eight examples of widespread false beliefs concerning autism spectrum disorder: 1. **Autism spectrum disorder (ASD) is a medical condition**. Autism is not a disease; it is a neurological **characteristic**. As a neurodevelopmental disorder, ASD indicates that a child's brain does not develop or operate normally in the same way as a "typical" child's brain. But **unique does not imply incorrect.** Consider the following:

1. Not every autistic person is unique. Some experts have even suggested that Leonardo da Vinci may have been somewhat neurodivergent. For anyone with this designation, that may be some small comfort since Leonardo was an incredibly

gifted genius in the arts, both painting and sculpting.

2. **Autism is a mental disorder.** Additionally, ASD is distinct from mental disorders in important ways. Schizophrenia and alcohol use disorder are two among the many mental diseases that typically manifest in later life. Conversely, *autism spectrum disorder (ASD) is a genetic disorder.* Treatments for mental illness are well-established in the medical community. Unfortunately, for autism, there is no "cure" since it doesn't meet any of the criteria that would necessitate a cure.

3. **An epidemic of autism is taking place**. Everyone knows what autism spectrum disorder is now. The availability and quality of services for children with autism are increasing in tandem with the public's understanding of the disorder. It may be that many persons with autism were never considered such and, therefore, never a part of any statistical analysis. In fact, it may always have been there in these numbers, but never generated in databases, and now that it is, it appears there is more of it—not so?

4. **There is a gender bias in autism**. Although ASD is more common in boys than girls, *autism is not a gender-specific disorder*. Approximately 4% of boys are autistic, according to the research, whereas only 1% of girls fall into this category. However, recent research is indicating that more girls have autism than were diagnosed previously because of this bias.

5. **Classifying all individuals with autism the same**. Assuming that all autistic individuals have the same traits or challenges is incorrect. Some common misconceptions

about autistic persons include that they are *brilliant, aggressive, have intellectual or learning difficulties, lack empathy, have trouble forming relationships, have trouble communicating, and have trouble in the workplace or at home.*

6. **Vaccines given to children cause autism**. Conclusions were based on erroneous data. The claim that vaccines cause autism lacks any evidence from the scientific community. Although there is evidence to the contrary, many people persist on believing this myth.

7. **Autism is caused by bad parenting**. There is no correlation between autism and parenting techniques. The unfortunate reality is that this misconception continues to be perpetuated and used *to criticize and condemn parents*. The belief that autism could be caused by poor parenting is similar to the belief previously that schizophrenia was the result of a "refrigerator mother." It was felt that mothers who were cold and withdrawing had children who developed schizophrenia. That, also, is not true and today we know that schizophrenia is a developmental as well as potentially genetic disorder that is not involved with parenting style. Mothers, however, were condemned for this for decades.

How Autism May Occur

Biomarkers are signs of a condition's presence at a specific moment; they might be genes, proteins, metabolites, or other samples taken from the body. So far, autism has no recognized biomarkers. The fact that there are numerous possible causes of autism and that researchers often disregard the interplay between these factors has significantly impeded efforts to identify biomarkers.

Gut microorganisms *may serve as a biomarker for neurological disorders* like autism. Scientists are very interested in the gut-brain axis, which refers to the relationship between the two systems. Immunity, neurotransmitter balance, digestive health, and countless other aspects of health are profoundly impacted by gut microorganisms.

A study conducted in Sweden **monitored parents and almost 17,000 children** born between 1997 and 1999 from the moment they were born. By the age of 23, roughly 1,200 of these youngsters had been diagnosed with a neurodevelopmental condition.

Prior to the onset of neurodevelopmental symptoms like irritability and sleep disturbances, as well as official medical diagnoses, there were *notable variations in bacterial composition and metabolite levels.* Autistic spectrum disorder, attention deficit hyperactivity disorder, and speech difficulties were among the numerous disorders in this sample study. It would appear that there is a great deal of variation in the microorganisms and metabolites that impact immunological and brain health in the umbilical cord blood and feces of newborns and children around the age of one. An increased risk *of autism was found in children with microbial imbalances* and a history of ***antibiotic overuse***.

What is one thing that antibiotics do that is usually not understood? They kill much *of the gut bacteria* that is important in the gut-brain interaction. How many parents are told to *replace the "good bacteria"* after antibiotic use? I would suggest that this is lacking in healthcare. A compromised immune system or impaired brain development, both of which are impacted by the gut microbiota, may be indicated by a history of antibiotic usage in early life.

But do we know definitively if either early antibiotic use or some other prenatal condition in the gut may have contributed to the development of autism? It seems the jury is still out on this question as well as many others. But it is a start in seeking answers to questions that have a major impact on a child and an adult's life.

Everything must be considered in the face of current, replicable research, and not myths that only serve to hurt others. Myth should be kept to fairytales and not science.

Chapter 9: Danger Hides in Diet Sodas--Can They Be Addictive?

Weight isn't only an entrenched obsession from a beauty-cultural perspective, but it is a definite health concern for millions. Looking at TV shows that feature individuals who weigh over 600 lbs. and are now seeking remedies by dieting and surgery serves as an example of how serious weight can become. Of course, these individuals may have stress-related or personality characteristics that drive them to eat excessively, and then there are those around them who contribute to the weight issues.

In addition to obesity, many adults suffer from other severe chronic conditions. An *increased risk of cardiovascular disease* is associated with hypertension, which **58% of overweight adults in the United States have.** Nearly a quarter of overweight persons in the United States also have **diabetes**.

Both individuals and the healthcare system bear the financial burden of obesity-related medical expenses. Medical expenses for persons with obesity were $1,861 more per person in 2019 compared to adults with a healthy weight. There was an additional outlay of $3,097 for every adult who suffered from extreme obesity. The corresponding 2019 medical expenses **amount to about $173 billion**.

From 2017 to March 2020, 41.9% of adults in the United States were obese. Simultaneously, 9.2% of individuals in the United States were **severely obese**. More than **22 million persons are very obese**, and over 100 million adults are overweight. Individuals are considered obese if their *body mass index (BMI) is 30 or over.* A BMI of **40 or above is considered severe obesity.**

I recall consulting at a diet-drink program where primarily women who were determined to be obese (via the standard questionable BMI) had enrolled. The program put them on a diet drink and restricted them to about 900 calories a day. Unfortunately, they weren't informed of the cardiac risk from lowered potassium (essential for nerves), the potential for hirsutism (excessive hair on their arms), or their spouses' attempts to sabotage their weight loss. One woman's husband kept bringing home high-calorie cakes and pizzas, and she found it difficult to resist them.

What happened? It upended their lives as when one woman went on a cruise and had to refrain from the many eating pleasures to keep to her drink, which she brought with her. They lost weight, but it caused difficulties in interpersonal relationships. Turning down invitations to celebrations became common.

For many attempting to seek some relief from high-caloric drinks and still maintain access to these often bubbly drinks, diet soda has become their beverage of choice. However, diet soda is *nutritionally worthless.* Additionally, it *includes artificial sweeteners*, whose effects on health have been the subject of *conflicting studies*. Consuming multiple servings daily raises concerns about its potential "toxicity."

What's the Problem with Diet Soda?

Although excessive consumption of diet soda has been seen as an addiction, the American Psychiatric Association disagrees. While many have attempted and failed to abstain from caffeine, artificial sweeteners, and diet soda, the APA *does not recognize these addictions.* Is it possible to get addicted to diet soda?

To provide a sugary taste without the sugar, diet sodas and other food products use aspartame, a substance that has mixed data related to cancer risk. After several **studies failed to provide proof of association**, international committees have, nevertheless, come to one conclusion: **limit their intake.**

To be at potential risk, a guideline was developed. An adult weighing 154.32 pounds would have to **drink more than 9–14 cans** of diet soft drink each day—assuming no other food sources—to surpass the permissible daily intake of aspartame, which is **200 or 300 mg in a can.** But there are other factors involved here, too, that contribute to continued consumption.

Limiting their consumption can be unmanageable *for some people*. What they develop is more of a habit with uncomfortable side effects if they cut back because of the caffeine in the drinks. The removal of both drink ingredients causes them to go through withdrawal. Caffeine and aspartame in diet sodas make them difficult to cut back on because, compared to sugar, artificial *sweeteners only stimulate the brain's reward system to a lesser extent*, making people need more.

Is this an addiction? Not in the sense that psychiatrists have considered it. It's more of **a compulsion**, but it does hit that reward center, and isn't that what addictive substances do?

The bottom line seems to be that diet sodas won't kill you, but they may have a downside that needs to be considered. Would it be better to drink water rather than soda with our meals?

Chapter 10: Survival and Healing When Natural Disasters Strike

O ur warming earth is experiencing *unanticipated, catastrophic changes* in weather that have and will continue to affect every aspect of our lives, especially our mental health, and we need to begin to understand what is at risk and how to cope.

In all, 403 weather and climate catastrophes have occurred in the United States since 1980, with damages and expenses above $1 billion. The sum of these 403 occurrences is more than $2.915 trillion. The recent wildfires in California alone, never mind the rest of the country, are expected to account for over $250 billion for rebuilding and assistance to the local population. In addition to the climate changes, there are economic changes, social disruptions, and a general feeling, often, of hopelessness or helplessness. But there is help, and there is hope even in the most dire of times.

Research conducted in 2024 suggests that to cope with natural disasters, people should seek professional help when needed, communicate openly about what happened, keep social connections with loved ones, practice self-care routines, limit their exposure to graphic disaster imagery, and be proactive in preparing for the event. It is important to recognize that vulnerable populations within affected communities have unique needs.

Many disasters have negative effects on people's mental health, and the World Risk Report (2024) notes that this is **especially true for women** and other **vulnerable groups**. Some of these are:

1. Post-Traumatic Stress Disorder (PTSD) is more common because people are impacted by disasters. Unfortunately, this is one disorder that can linger for quite a long time and will need therapeutic intervention, both of a verbal and, possibly, pharmacologic types.

2. During and after catastrophes, there is a higher incidence of sexual, *interpersonal, and gender-specific violence*, which can have a devastating impact on the mental health of women and marginalized groups. When people are feeling extremely stressed, it is difficult to control anger, and to displace onto others around us. Recognize this, and you have not only helped yourself, but your community, your family and anyone in your area. Recognition and self-control are two things that are vital during these times.

3. The disruption of sexual and reproductive healthcare services caused by disasters can lead to an increase in the *incidence of sexually transmitted diseases and unplanned pregnancies*, as well as increased mental health stress.

4. Putting men and boys first in the food chain can have negative effects on women and girls' mental health by *reducing their food intake and increasing their risk of nutritional deficiencies.* How should food resources be equitably distributed in order to maintain a community? Sexual bias helps no one.

5. Economic difficulties and increased household responsibilities can push children, particularly *girls, to drop out of school*, which can have a negative impact on their mental health. If education is disrupted, careers are stunted, and the potential of children is limited. This has an effect on everyone. Education is essential and finding the means to maintain it even during natural disasters is highly important.

6. More chance of early or forced marriage: Natural disasters increase the likelihood of *child marriage and forced marriage*, both of which can impact mental health in the long run.

7. Traditional masculine duties and the stigma associated with asking for or receiving assistance may contribute to an *increased suicide rate* among males.

8. There is an *increased risk of injury and related mental health disorders* for men since they are more likely to work in disaster management and reconstruction.

The Way Forward

Recovering from any natural disaster involves, in part, accepting that the life you had before will undergo change according to what has been affected in your area. Change, of course, means new housing arrangements, new neighborhoods or towns, a change in job location or career aspirations, and **plans for the future**. Some of it will seem daunting, and most of it will require that you *deal with a sense of loss or grief* over what has happened.

Each person will go through the grieving process in their own way because grieving is natural and personal, so there are no specific steps for grieving normally." The stages were arbitrary and based on a very small sample of dying patients and the researcher's personal observations. It was subjective.

Having a strong sense of community can help with the hardship of recovering from sudden disasters. When the time comes to begin the next phase of recovery—which may involve negotiating with insurance companies or even relocating—affected people might consider *adopting new customs and gathering new sentimental objects* to help them get through it.

In the aftermath of a tragedy, *having a community* of others who have been through the same thing can be a great comfort. **Isolation is a significant obstacle** to overcoming hardships. Sharing information and resources within a tight-knit community of neighbors and friends can also help determine what to do in the aftermath of a crisis. If ever there was a time for togetherness, it would be after a natural or man-made disaster.

Each of us may have specific ways that we cope with adversity, but there are a number of accepted ways for the greater majority of persons in our culture, and these need to be considered, too. Some of them are fairly obvious, and others may be something that requires a change in your daily routine. Consider each of them carefully and see where some of them may prove helpful and which should be included in your survival after any disaster.

Tips on Personal Coping

Preparation, self-care, and establishing support networks are coping mechanisms. Here are some ways that you or someone you care about can cope:

1. **Ensure your well-being** as you are ensuring that of others. Self-care isn't selfish; it's the thing to do to survive. If you need a "time

out," take it in order to continue going on and see it as necessary, not that you are unwilling to help others.

2. **Maintain a balanced diet**, stay away from drugs and alcohol, and release stress with exercise (even if it is only a short stroll or some deep breathing).

3. **Get in touch** with loved ones. Communication with others is one way to reinforce our ability to maintain our health, so reach out and relate.

4. **Discuss your emotions** with a reliable person. Make sure your kids know it's alright to cry if needed.

5. *Keep informed as to what you need to know* about the disaster, but lessen your intake of news. A person's anxiety levels can rise, and the event may be relived in their minds due to the constant news coverage. Constantly going over something in your mind, rather than helping you cope, can reinforce that negative experience to your detriment. You can begin to be your own coach with self-soothing messages that you give to yourself silently. Tell yourself that it is going to be OK, that you can get through this, that you need to rest your body and your mind, and that there are others who share your sentiments and who will be there for you.

6. Sleep is **important**, even though it is difficult under some circumstances to sleep. But understand that getting proper sleep and rest is important for your physical and mental health, and you owe it to yourself. To get a better night's rest, cut out coffee, electronics, and alcohol at least an hour before bedtime.

7. Create a **schedule**. Maintain consistent eating patterns. Ensure that there are enjoyable pursuits to anticipate. Schedules provide structure and when all your normal structure has been disrupted, you need to recreate structure for yourself. Yes, it may seem a bit rigid, but structure is key to progressing through this disaster.

8. **Delay making life-altering choices**. Often, in these types of circumstances, rash judgments may mean poor outcomes in the future. Give yourself time to consider carefully once you have sufficient information, and then *discuss plans and changes with reliable sources*. Managing major changes, such as a change in careers following a calamity, can be challenging, so be prepared to consider changes that may require additional training and how you might be able to access that training. Often, areas needing it most, such as those recovering from natural disasters, offer training programs, and individuals can also receive grants for this training.

9. Be prepared **for changes—they** will come, undoubtedly. Disasters can cause long-term disruptions to people's lives, such as the loss of their houses, schools, or jobs. **Allow yourself plenty of time to heal**.

10. Tackle pet **care**. Assisting with emotional rehabilitation with animals can be helpful. Pets also serve as great emotional sources because they show us undeniable, unquestioning love, and in caring for them, we maintain a sense of responsibility that can help us through difficult times.

11. Help in **homeless shelters** or go outside when the weather permits. **A sense of purpose** like this at difficult times can be helpful to you, as you can be helpful to others. We don't need research to tell us that caring for others and engaging in charity helps the caregiver and the charitable as well as those who receive it. There is a great deal of research evidence pointing to this. Charitable work also provides that vital sense of purpose that is most important to us. 12. **Be wary of someone who exhibits symptoms of substance abuse,** sadness, anxiety, or chronic stress. If you are having trouble managing your emotional distress, it is time to seek help.

13. **Join a group** that will encourage you. People can feel less alone and more supported in a support group setting. Understanding that others are in the same place as you and are going through the same emotional upheaval's can be helpful. Take advantage of it and share with others and allow them to share with you.

14. **Talk to a trusted, well-known financial advisor.** Money worries could arise after losing a job or a property. With the assistance of a financial consultant, you can make plans and gain access to assets.

Climate change means a new world going forward, as all of us have come to realize. This doesn't mean that life can't be pleasant, or we can't experience many of the things that we enjoy, but there will be change. *Adopting a more positive attitude* is one of the most important things you can do for yourself and for those you love.

Chapter 11: Wildfire Smoke Linked to Dementia, Brain and Body Health, So Beware

The number of acres burned by wildfires every year **has almost doubled since 1985**. And the smoke from these fires now regularly pollutes the air for most of the country. It's not simply smoke but many harmful chemicals because it comes from different types of fuels (like homes, cars, biomass, etc.). Problems with the *heart, lungs,* *eyes, nose*, and, more recently, the **brain** have been **linked to wildfire exposure**.

Both short-term and long-term exposure to wildfire smoke and other pollutants like ozone and diesel emissions can cause *inflammation in the brain*. We believe pollutants in the lungs, too, cause neurological effects. Previous research has suggested that breathing in particulate matter (PM) causes pulmonary proteolysis, creating fragmented molecules that *enter the bloodstream and weaken the blood–brain barrier* (BBB). As we know, the blood-brain barrier is vital to maintaining the brain's integrity and keeping it functioning as we require, but once this barrier is breached, danger enters with whatever crosses over it, and smoke seems to be one of the vehicles for this.

Climate Central, a nonprofit group, says that every person in the US took in more harmful wildfire smoke in 2023 than in any other year since 2006. Studies show that over the last ten years, **exposure has grown 27 times in the United States.**

Pollutants from wildfire smoke are mixed together, but fine particulate matter (PM2.5) makes up most of it and is a **significant health risk**. A study of more than 1.2 million people in Southern California shows that smoke seems to be one of the vehicles for this. But it's not just the normal effect on the lungs that we would expect to see from wildfire smoke since it has been found to have a previously unknown danger. Over the course of ten years, it was found that wildfire smoke **raises the chance of dementia** more than any other type of air pollution. Researchers indicate that wildfire smoke is more dangerous **to brain health** than other types of air pollution.

Fine particulate matter (PM2.5) is air pollution from *industry, cars, and wildfire smoke*. These are very small drops of *solid and liquid matter* in the air, *30 times smaller than the width of a human hair*. The chance of getting dementia was much higher when people were exposed to PM2.5 from wildfire smoke than when people were exposed to other sources of air pollution. While smoke from other sources increases the risk of dementia, it is **not as much as smoke from wildfires**.

Mental Health Consequences

On days with excessive pollution, more people go to the hospital for depression, suicide attempts, and psychotic episodes. Study after study shows that children whose **mothers were expose**d to high amounts of particulates while they were pregnant are *more likely to have motor and cognitive problems as adults.* These studies, therefore, indicate the vulnerability of the unborn baby and the ease of entry through the placenta of these toxins.

One study is one of the first to look at the effects of particulate matter on teens, whose brains are still growing. Teens have enough problems to deal with in their adjustment to approaching maturity, but when we add wildfire smoke and this type of particulate into the mix, complications, especially of an emotional type, arise.

Data from 10,000 pre-teens in the Adolescent Brain Cognitive Development Study (ABCD), the largest US child health study, was analyzed. Two of the 21 study sites are at the University of Colorado at Boulder. Researchers looked at parent questionnaires from four different times over three years and found that for both boys and girls, *each extra day of exposure at unsafe levels increased the chance that they would have depression, anxiety, and other "internalizing symptoms" up to a year later.* So the damage may not show initially, but it may come after a period of time, and, seemingly, it would not be connected to the wildfire smoke—but it is that smoke that may have caused it.

But wildfire smoke doesn't only affect the immediate area. While the exact distance depends on the wind and weather, smoke from wildfires can move hundreds of miles. This wide area has an effect on the air quality in places far from the fire, and the *effects can last for weeks*. Smoke from wildfires, as previously noted, can have a significant effect on health. Some of the chemicals and small particles in smoke can impact the eyes, nose, and throat, making it difficult to breathe, cough, and wheeze. If someone already has a breathing problem, like asthma, these symptoms can get worse.

How Can You Protect Yourself

It's important to remember how the air quality is affected by the flames in the area, even if you are miles away. These are some simple things you can do to stay away from smoke and clean the air in your home and car.

1. Spend as much time as possible inside Do not go outside as much, especially if you are working out when the air quality is poor. Inside is the best place to be when there is smoke. Keep a close eye on local news on air quality. They often include a color-coded Air Quality Index (AQI) to help you decide how active you should be.

2. Close all the doors and windows All of your windows and doors should be closed to keep smoke out of your home. Weather stripping or towels can fill in holes under doors and windows if you can. If your whole-house fan or window air conditioner does not have a HEPA filter, do not use them. They can bring smoke inside.

3. Use an air cleaner If you have an air cleaner, especially one with a HEPA filter, use it to help clean the air inside your home. You might want to use portable air cleaners in the bedrooms and living rooms where you spend the most time. ***Do not use things that make ozone*** because it can make the air quality worse. When purchasing an air filter, carefully read the instructions and **see whether or not it produces ozone**. If it does, you don't want it, and I would suggest that you do a search on the Internet for the most effective air cleaners on the market without ozone-producing elements. Remember, ozone

is bad for our planet's outside protective covering, and it's bad in your home.

4. Create a room with clean air Set aside one room as a "clean air room" if keeping your whole house smoke-free is hard. The HEPA air filter should be set up in a room with few windows and doors. During times of intense. smoke, spend most of your time in this room.

5. Know how to use your air conditioner If you have an air conditioner, make sure it is set not to bring in air from outside and move it inside. Keep the windows closed and, in your car, set your *air conditioner to the recycling mode* to keep smoke out of your car while you drive.

6. Stay away from things that make indoor pollution worse When the air quality outside is a concern, it is important to cut down on indoor pollution sources as well. *Do not use gas stoves, burn candles, or smoke inside.* The air quality inside can get even worse, and these actions can make the environment more dangerous. Is it OK to use scented devices that put aromas into the air? Scientists are currently looking at this, and it may not be a good idea.

7. Put on a mask if you need to. If you have to go outside, wear a mask to keep out small particles. Wearing N95 respirators or KN95 masks can help protect you from dangerous particles in wildfire smoke. *Scarves or masks made of cloth will not keep smoke out.* In fact, bandannas are of no use whatsoever.

8. Drink plenty of water and look after your health It is important to stay hydrated because wildfire smoke can irritate your lungs and make it harder to breathe. Your lungs and sinuses stay moist when you drink plenty of water. For people who already have conditions like asthma, make sure they have all of their medicines on hand. Also, do not wait to call their doctor if they have trouble breathing or other signs.

We are beginning to suffer through the effects of climate change and wildfires as a result. Living with these conflagrations may mean changes over a long period of time because climate change will be with us for decades, if not longer. Lifestyle changes are mandated if we expect to maintain our health when we need to deal with wildfire-induced pollution.

Chapter 12: When the Going Is Rough, Here's How to Get Going

Not every day starts out on a positive note, and for most of us, if not all, there will be rougher days than others for getting going. But there are always ways to help ourselves, and that's the secret to providing what we need to carry on. It may seem prosaic, but the saying *"When the going gets tough, the tough get going"* is apt here, and we must adhere to it. If not, we decide our future in a less-than-positive manner: no blame here, just techniques to help yourself. Starting is hard, but it gets easier.

There is mounting evidence that practicing gratitude improves mental and physical well-being. This includes fewer depressive symptoms, more positive affect and life satisfaction, better sleep, and more engagement in health behaviors.

Research evidence suggests that there may be *psychological and physiological changes* associated with an increase in gratitude, which in turn affects one's well-being by drawing our focus more strongly to positive experiences and **encouraging a more optimistic interpretation and memory of past events**. Similarly, research has shown that being grateful boosts social support, which in turn improves the quality of relationships and overall health.

Gratitude interventions show promise as a supplemental, even self-therapy, for mental health. Each of us is, in one sense or another, is our own therapist, and each of us has the power to make small but significant changes. Every change can lead to a more fulfilling, happier life. Wouldn't you want that? Even in the darkest times, this method can be your guiding light. Hold that light high and allow it to brighten the darkness around you.

<u>What Can You Do?</u>

There are two ways to think about gratitude: as *a quality and as a condition*. People typically describe thankfulness as "*a generalized inclination to recognize and respond with thankful emotion to the wonderful occurrences in life*," viewing it as a trait or disposition.

There are **two parts** to the practice of gratitude: **first**, being aware that you have had a good experience; and **second**, attributing that good fortune to something outside of yourself, such as other people, your surroundings, or an intangible thing. According to the ideas provided by research, a *sense of purpose, a healthy lifestyle, and prosocial activities* are all promoted by good emotions like thankfulness. Participating in these pursuits helps mental, physical, and social resources flourish, **setting in motion a domino effect** that eventually *improves one's health.*

You could think of gratitude as a state of mind as well as a character attribute. The term *"deviational gratitude"* describes a person's **innate propensity** to notice and respond with grateful emotion to the fortunate occurrences in life. Feelings of gratitude are more common among people who naturally have an appreciative attitude. There once was a highly popular newspaper cartoon character who viewed everything in a negative light, and he **had a perpetual raining cloud over his head**. We can choose to be that character, or we can choose to be someone who views things in a more positive light.

But there are more benefits to this specific type of orientation, other than in our mental health, and they are involved in **overall physical health**. Studies observed a small but statistically significant effect of gratitude on stress and inflammation biomarkers. This small but statistically significant decrease in total inflammatory biomarker concentrations was observed **in a group of heart disease patients** who participated in an 8-week **thankfulness journaling** intervention as compared to a control group that received standard care. Another research project indicated that thankfulness had minor impacts on tumor necrosis in the blood but no such effects on other inflammatory biomarkers. The results of a different randomized controlled trial on the effects of gratitude diaries on salivary cortisol levels were inconclusive. Further research is necessary to clarify these findings, although these mixed results may indicate that thankfulness may have some beneficial impacts on stress and inflammation biomarkers.

Evidence suggests that practicing gratitude improves the quality of sleep one gets. Gratitude therapies, such as keeping **a gratitude diary**, have been shown in multiple trials to enhance the quality of sleep. Consider this study: after two weeks of thankfulness journaling, participants' daily sleep quality increased considerably compared to the control group that did not receive any treatment.

Another study compared a **thankfulness journaling intervention** to a waitlist control condition and found that sleep quality improved moderately between the two. Not only that, but a randomized pilot study found that **practicing thankfulness before bed each night** improved both the quality and length of sleep, as well as reduced pre-sleep arousal. Although the benefits may differ based on the particular intervention and comparative settings, on average, thankfulness treatments improve the quality of sleep.

Today, you may find it hard to find some things for which you can be thankful, but give yourself some time and pull up those memories you have stored inside you. *There have been instances in your life* where either you have prevailed over adversity or someone else has extended some kindness to you.

Look for the kindness; look for the strength you had and have, and you will find what you need to carry on. As I've always said, something good can come from even the worst of circumstances. I am not being a Pollyanna, but I am **encouraging you to seek** instead of slumping back in your seat and accepting. Why not consider starting a gratitude journal for yourself? Remember, you can be grateful for small things and it doesn't have to be anything major like you got a wonderful promotion. It can be that you got up today and the sun was shining, or something small happened that you neglected to notice was really a good thing. Look around you and you will find things to be grateful for, so mark them down in your journal and be sure to refer back to them whenever you're feeling a bit down. It will help you, it will help you sleep, and it will reduce your stress and your outlook on life. If we don't reinforce the good things in our life, what are we doing?

Chapter 13: Fermented Foods Pack a Punch in Cancer Prevention and Health of Your Microbiome

C ancer is one of our most distressing diseases, where, while some may be treated to effect with current therapies, others remain resistant, and researchers have been seeking ways to help patients, prior to developing cancers, to build up their own potential resistance to many forms.

Twenty million people were diagnosed with cancer in 2022, with 9.7 million **losing their lives to the disease**. Within five years of receiving a cancer diagnosis, an estimated 53.5 million people were still alive. *Cancer affects around 1 in 5 individuals* at some point in their lives, and it claims the lives of around 1 in 9 men and 1 in 12 women. Now, there seems to be a connection that may be valuable in treating cancer and other diseases.

Numerous chronic diseases, including the development and progression of various cancers, are mechanistically associated with the gut microbiome, which is composed of trillions of bacteria, viruses, fungi, yeast, protozoans, and archaea. *Head and neck cancer patients, those with colorectal cancer, inflammatory bowel disease, type 1 diabetes, obesity, and celiac disease all have decreased gut microbial diversity.* The gut microbiome can be affected by a variety of changeable factors, making it an intriguing biological **target for cancer prevention and treatment.**

One crucial possibility to increase response to immunotherapies and overall cancer survivability is through dietary **interventions** that affect the gut microbiota, potentially improving anti-cancer immunity. Promisingly, eating fermented foods can enhance immunity by *changing the makeup of the gut microbiota.* But there are certain restrictions that need to be applied to including fermented foods in your diet, and we have listed them below.

History tells us that fermentation by microbes existing in the source material or processing environment has been used to make fermented foods for a long time. The fermentation process, the byproducts of these microbes, and the fluctuating pH of the raw material inhibited the growth of harmful bacteria. Therefore, originally intended to provide a means of preserving foods, especially in areas where famine may occur, this processing has additional benefits related to our health.

Things to Think About

Just like any food, improperly produced fermented goods might pose risks. Inadequate production hygiene or the use of contaminated materials are the primary causes of worry. Making or storing fermented foods in an unsanitary environment can lead to the growth of dangerous bacteria rather than beneficial ones. In the case of handmade or small-batch goods, when quality control is more likely to be lax, this is particularly the case.

Depending on how they are made, fermented foods can include dangerous amounts of chemicals that can make you ill. That is why it is critical to stick to food safety regulations while manufacturing your own or purchasing from reputable suppliers. Modern food safety regulations ensure the quality and safety of fermented foods, even those with a history of safe preparation spanning millennia.

Even though the *gut microbiome in our bodies might benefit* from fermented foods, there are a number of individuals who should exercise caution **regarding these foods.** The majority of people may eat fermented foods without worry, and they may have significant health benefits. But before you start eating more fermented foods, talk to your doctor if you have a *histamine intolerance, weakened immune system, or gastrointestinal issue.* It goes without saying that the **elderly, pregnant women, and babies** should all be careful with fermented foods. It is advisable, if at all, to consume fermented foods in moderation at all times.

Besides those sensitive to these foods, there are **specific medications** that indicate fermented foods would be dangerous for them to take along with these prescriptions. In fact, they **can cause severe side**

effects. But an additional word of caution is advisable here. There are specific differences *between probiotics and fermented foods.*

"Probiotic foods" or "containing probiotics" are terms that describe or label fermented drinks and foods. By making these claims, manufacturers may be trying to tell people that their products include live, healthy microbes. *We should only use the word "probiotic" when the health benefits of specific living microorganisms are proven.* There has to be more going on than just the nutritional value of the food matrix for the health benefit to be because of the active microbes.

Commercially available fermented foods probably do not qualify as "probiotic" fermented foods most of the time. So far, there has been **no evidence that fermented foods and drinks have any health benefits**, and they often contain microbial consortia that are not clearly defined but at varying quantities.

Salads, Pickles, and Fermented Foods with MAIOs

Patients on monoamine oxidase inhibitors (MAOIs) and specific drugs for Parkinson's disease have been linked to a potentially fatal rise in blood pressure, and this food category includes *tyramine.* Certain fermented foods might interact with monoamine oxidase inhibitors (MAOIs) in a way that can cause hazardous adverse effects. Anyone with hypertension would be advised to regard these foods as potentially dangerous for them.

The foods can cause headaches, rapid or irregular heartbeat, sleepiness, chest discomfort, or disorientation. Serious health complications like stroke, heart attack, or organ damage can result from a fast rise in blood pressure caused by consuming an excessive amount of tyramine while taking an MAOI. Foods rich in tyramine include *aged cheeses, cured meats, fermented soy products (such as miso and soy sauce), sauerkraut, and draft beer*, which can interact dangerously with MAOIs. It's important to remember that foods, just as medications, can cause side effects, especially when we are not exercising appropriate care in the selection of what we eat. No one should take the matter of an MAOI medication lightly when considering dietary items. If you have any questions about any of the food items that should be excluded from your diet when on these medications, please confirm with your healthcare provider and a nutritionist or certified/licensed dietitian for some guidance.

All in all, as in many things, fermented foods may play a role in maintaining a healthy gut microbiome. Still, we must be conscientious in selecting our foods and carefully reading food labels. Remember, everything on the label may not contain everything in the product, but if you are taking medication or are in the above-named group at potential risk, think twice. As in everything, consult your healthcare provider for advice on your diet. You may love pickles or soyo kimchi, but it may not be in the cards for you because of the potential for adverse side effects. Find something else.

Chapter 14: The Lawn You Love Is Killing Your Mental Health by Your Pesticide Use

A lush, green lawn was once thought to be a desirable sign of having made it and attained the American dream—a home of one's own. But research regarding how we maintain those lawns and what they truly cost in terms of our mental health and that of our families provides a shocking fact: they can be lethal to us. Numerous studies over the last two decades have demonstrated links between pesticide exposure and conditions affecting the brain and mental health, such as Parkinson's disease, **Attention Deficit Hyperactivity Disorder (ADHD), depression, and dementia**.

When it comes to agricultural workers or people working in land-scaping, the effects are even more dire. Setting out to spray away the dreadful pests that chew up our bushes and attack those green carpets that front our homes, these workers are putting themselves at risk of not simply mental health difficulties, but serious health impairments. How many landscapers have you seen wearing protective clothing?

All functional groups (studied), as well as pesticide classes like organochlorines, organophosphates, and carbamates, were significantly associated with a higher risk of probable mental disorder based on exposure duration, frequency, personal protective equipment usage, and hygienic behavior.

Children cavorting on the lawn, playing catch, racing around with the family dog, or eating foods sprayed with these chemicals *are receiving heavy doses* of these dangerous materials, as research has shown. How do these sprays kill insects? They are neurotoxic, so do you believe they wouldn't have some effect on us or our kids? Of course, they would, and it is neurotoxicity that portends the greatest danger, especially in *developing brains of children.*

A database of pesticide-induced disorders or illnesses is currently maintained and indicates that the problems range from **asthma, autism, learning disabilities, birth defects, reproductive dysfunction, diabetes, Parkinson's and Alzheimer's diseases, and several types of cancer.**

But the damage may be even more far-reaching in areas of our bodies that are not immediately evident. There is now concern that our microbiota-gut-brain axis may be in danger. We are now learning the important influence this connection plays on our brains and behavior.

How did it get into our brains? High levels of specific pesticides have been found in the soil, and they can then enter our bodies through the food we eat, the air we breathe, or even our skin.

The nose, by the way, is an excellent vehicle for bringing in toxins since it is intimately associated with the brain. Why do you suppose there are new medications being formulated in the form of nose sprays? It's because the nose is one wonderful way to get things into the brain and the blood. If we introduce a medication via the nose, we miss what is known as the "first pass," which means the blood going through the liver where it is rendered less potent, so avoiding this first pass and going to the nose maintains the strength of the medication. Some research has indicated that the first pass can remove as much as 70% of the potency of a medication.

Consider, however, that pesticides do not remain in your lawn but are washed away with sprinklers or rain and then go into the groundwater and, perhaps, into the drinking water in your area. The cycle may begin on the lawn, but it doesn't end there.

Chapter 15: Dancing and Meditation All Rolled Into One

M editation can be a wonderful source of stress relief and even creativity, but it has a usually prescribed series of poses (especially in yoga) that must be maintained during the meditation. The prescription of posing denies the body's ability to utilize other forms of stress reduction at the same time, and now we are beginning to realize that combining both meditation (yoga and other forms) with free-form dancing may have the potential to increase the power that they both have for stress reduction and creativity. Research is now probing this area as a potential new resource for assistance that will mean both body and brain health-promoting activities.

Findings from a comprehensive analysis of qualitative and quantitative research point to several associations between mindfulness training and improved mental health. Beginning to see that dancing mindfulness promotes holistic wellness through dance and mindfulness meditation.

Dance/movement therapy (DMT) aims to improve health and well-being by integrating the individual's emotional, social, cognitive, and physical selves through movement. Through creative processes and interactive activities, DMT promotes physical functioning, *psychological health, self-efficacy, and social connectedness.* A key component of DMT is psychoeducation and **cognitive processing,** which helps people incorporate somatic insights and corrective feedback into their cognitive awareness for better mental and behavioral health.

Not only is this combined therapeutic intervention feasible for anyone experiencing higher stress, but it also applies to individuals who are experiencing pain, such as **chronic lower back pain**. People suffering from persistent lower back pain participated in a 12-week group intervention, and they reported *numerous positive outcomes*. We know that pain is a major impediment not only to lifestyle but also to our psychological outlook on activity and inhibits individuals in many areas. Therefore, modalities that would address physical and psychological aspects are of utmost importance. One thing to remember, here is that self-report is not necessarily a reliable means of evaluating anything. There is no robust scale for this, and it simply means people are saying, possibly, what they believe the researcher wants to hear or just doing something made them feel better.

Over half of the people who participated in the study reported a *significant improvement in their cLBP (chronic low back pain)-related symptoms,* emotional well-being, and ability to participate in daily activities due to the treatment. The decrease in pain catastrophizing and fear-avoidance tendencies was also associated with higher motivation and readiness to actively participate in movement and exercise, consistent with previous findings. The fear-avoidance paradigm highlights the central significance of fear-avoidance attitudes in maintaining and worsening chronic pain disorders, making the findings even more significant within that framework. The end result was that people were able to anticipate activities without this chronic fear avoidance because they had an opportunity to see that they were still able to function in some way that helped them.

All measures related to the study, however, were self-reported, as I noted above, and it is impossible to provide solid evidence for these reports. i.e., no psychological data associated with pain or scales for pain before and after the study. Unfortunately, pain scales have proven to be inadequate in their efficacy.

What seems to be apparent, however, is that *individuals can benefit from a more comprehensive approach to pain management* if group therapy incorporates mindfulness practices with expressive and creative movement/dance-based strategies. As a result, they can actively manage their discomfort and improve their physical and mental health.

Additional studies with Parkinson's (PD) patients involved in such multimodal movement and meditation programs have also proven helpful in improving their quality of life. According to another study, individuals with PD showed improvements in *motor and nonmotor symptom severity,* ADLs, balance, and overall health after two years of community-based dancing courses.

Is dancing the answer? Dance may help with physical and mental symptoms, studies suggest. Extending on this research, on a personal level, would seem to show that music may also aid daily life. We know that music plays a role in mood, and when incorporating it with dance movements, whichever ones you wish, it may be key to helping many people who are looking for simple, self-help measures. Why not give it a try?

Chapter 16: Panic Attacks While Sleeping Are Possible, and You May Be Having Them

R esearch shows panic attack symptoms are similar, whether awake or asleep. But night terrors can be defined by differences in how severe and frequent these signs are experienced. However, individuals experiencing *daytime panic* attacks tend to *describe more physical manifestations*, such as racing thoughts and feelings *of chest tightness or suffocation.*

Daytime panic seems linked to fearful thoughts, unlike nighttime attacks, suggesting a *mental, not biological, explanation for nocturnal episodes.* You can find it difficult to breathe, experience a rapid heartbeat, and perspire heavily. Nocturnal panic attacks are more common in those with panic disorder or panic attacks. But the number of symptoms of nocturnal panic attacks is wide-ranging and somewhat troubling both to the patient and those who are diagnosing any disorder because of the diversity.

Nocturnal panic disorder is characterized by waking up in the middle of the night feeling extremely afraid or uncomfortable, with accompanying cognitive and somatic signs of arousal. Palpitations, a racing heart, or an increased heart rate; perspiration; shakiness or trembling; feelings of suffocation or difficulty breathing; choking sensations; chest pain or discomfort; nausea or abdominal distress; dizziness, unsteadiness, lightheadedness, or fainting; chills or heat sensations; paresthesias, or numbness or tingling; depersonalization, or a sense of detachment from oneself; fear of losing control, or "going crazy," and, finally, a fear of death.

Despite the abundance of symptoms, there is little difference between panic attacks that happen while awake and those that happen throughout the night. However, the number of symptoms can lead to difficulty in diagnosis.

We know how *panic attacks during the day can disrupt our lives,* even the lives of people we would assume are free from such episodes, but that's not the case. Who is one famous person admitting to discomforting anxiety attacks, and how have they affected her life? It's Kendall Jenner. Well-known and successful actors have, at various times, admitted that they are victims of panic attacks, often just before a performance. Of course, this could be thought of as performance anxiety, but their panic is almost crippling. I heard of one famous singer who downed a pint of alcohol before she had to go on stage.

But what about panic attacks over which we seemingly have no control and that come upon us as we are sleeping? This remains a problem for patients and healthcare. There seem to be **many explanations offered**, and they are varied from *biological to unconscious to what we eat and even to stomach upset.* Can we lay the blame for them on one thing? Probably not because they may have many things that caused them to occur, and for each, there has to be a definitive solution.

The clinician must take an appropriate history in order to make the diagnosis. Potentially *useful are multidisciplinary treatments* that include neurologists and psychiatrists, as well as methods to track the patient's reaction to treatment. *Creating a standardized method* to distinguish nocturnal panic disorder from other sleep-related illnesses could be a way to advance this area of study.

There is usually no obvious cause or explanation when you awaken with a panic episode. Some of the symptoms may be the same as those of a daylight panic attack. On the other hand, since **our brains do not "turn off"** while we sleep, any concerns or worries that we have been carrying around with us during the day **may resurface while we are sleeping** and trigger a panic attack when we wake up. Additionally, if you have trouble controlling your panic attacks during the day, you are more likely to have them during the night.

Handling Nighttime Panic Attacks

There are several things that experts suggest you can do if you awaken with a panic attack at night, and they include:

1. If you wake up in the middle of a panic attack, it is crucial that you do not try to force yourself to stop or resist the attack. Recognize

the panic attack for what it is. *Keep in mind that this is just transitory* and will pass. You must simply allow things to transpire.

2. Reestablish a state of relaxation in your body by making an effort to relax. *Breathe normally by taking deep breaths* in and out gently. Untense your muscles and direct your attention to pleasant mental imagery.

3. If you are having a panic attack and can not seem to get back to sleep, it's best to distract yourself from the terror by getting up and doing something. Arouse yourself physically and get out of bed. If you are having trouble refocusing, try some *yoga stretches, some soft music, a motivational book, or even something as mundane as ironing.*

4. Retire to your bed only when you are absolutely exhausted; do not return to your bed until you are ready to sleep again. If you are having trouble relaxing while lying in bed, try breathing deeply *in through your nose and out through your mouth*. Make sure your entire belly moves in rhythm with your breath, not just your chest.

5. To ensure you get a decent night's sleep, *give yourself plenty of time to wind down before bedtime.* A good rule of thumb is to get to bed at least eight hours before your alarm goes off. You can find yourself anxiously watching the clock and questioning if you will feel refreshed the following day if you stay up too late and do not give yourself enough time to sleep. Anxieties brought on by negative thinking can lead to a panic attack.

6. Many people have trouble sleeping because they are worried about *what is to come the next day,* so make sure you are ready for it. You can attempt to alleviate this worry by ensuring that you are well-prepared. A to-do list or an organized closet are two good examples.

7. Get into the habit of going to bed and waking up at around the same times each day. Try to *maintain a fairly consistent wake-up time* throughout the week, including on weekends.

8. If you suffer from nighttime anxiety and jitters, as well as trouble falling or staying asleep, cutting back *on sweets, coffee, and alcohol* before bed may help. I knew a very famous actor who told me that he had problems getting to sleep at night and had to drink almost 2 bottles of wine. As anyone will tell you, that is a very bad way to deal with sleeplessness. In fact, it causes more problems than it solves.

9. *Do not use any electronic devices,* including smartphones, tablets, and laptops, in the *hour or two* leading up to your intended bedtime. The light that these gadgets emit can be too stimulating and cause you to stay awake.

As you can see, there are a number of things you can do, and one of them is to realize that *you do have control over this*, and there are things you can do to help yourself. Of course, if you have repeated difficulties with nocturnal panic, and if any of your symptoms seem to be related to something of physical concern, you should be checked out by your physician and, possibly, someone specializing in sleep medicine.

In fact, it's always in your best interest to share these difficulties with your treating physician and to discuss potential future treatment. One caution should be that sleep medications are **not indicated on a chronic basis.** These medications, while useful for the short term, meaning one or two days, can bring on catastrophic results, as the research has shown.

Sleep medications, if used on a chronic (regular) basis, can have tragic results, as we have seen in numerous lawsuits related to them. As I recall, one woman who lived in the western part of the United States, was prescribed a sleep medication and took it regularly. The result? It caused a psychosis that resulted in her, shooting her aged mother to death on the mother's birthday. The woman walked into the mother's bedroom with a birthday cake and a loaded handgun and killed her.

This is not the only case that has been publicized in the professional literature.

One thing that we do notice is that a *regular schedule* and learning to relax, not only during the day but especially prior to going to sleep at night, is essential. Whatever way you decide to relax is something that you will determine and *one that works best for you*. There are many patients and professionals offering their ways of relaxing, but that **may not be what helps you**. If you need to get up to do a crossword puzzle or put a puzzle together or, as mentioned earlier, iron some clothes, that's fine. Even getting up and moving around and **regulating your breathing** will help.

Nocturnal panic attacks still present difficulties in diagnosis, but you do have power, and you can exercise it when you need to do it. And, as always, speak to your healthcare provider about any difficulties you may be having with sleep in general or panic.

Chapter 17: Decaf Unsafe or Not in Your Morning Tea or Coffee?

Waking up in the morning may mean reaching for a freshly brewed cup of coffee to help stimulate your nervous system and get you ready for the day. While some prefer coffee, others may choose tea; both beverages can contain caffeine or be decaffeinated, depending on your preference. But what's the *difference, besides caffeine*, between one with it and one without it, and is there any concern about removing caffeine from beverages? The primary difference is that one method uses a chemical **(methylene chloride), which** may be **banned** in other applications *but not in coffee.*

Recently, environmental advocacy organizations urged the United States Food and Drug Administration to think about banning this chemical, often used to produce decaf coffee. The EPA has **banned methylene chloride** due to its health risks, including *cancer and death*. One group calling for banning this chemical in coffee making is the non-profit Clean Label Project, which is fighting to find alternatives to methylene chloride in coffee decaffeination.

How Do They Remove Caffeine?

In the United States, the FDA (Food and Drug Administration) controls caffeine levels in coffee (methylene chloride in decaffeinated coffee to 10 parts per million), tea, and other products by setting limits that determine safe levels and permitted caffeine removal methods.

There are a few different ways to extract caffeine from plants. The most common *is methylene chloride*, also known as **the European method.** Another method employs ethyl acetate, sometimes called the "natural solvent" because it is found in many fruits such as sugarcane and bananas. The **Swisswater method uses hot water**, and the **carbon dioxide method** uses liquid carbon dioxide. This can change the coffee's chemical makeup and flavor depending on the process.

The most common **procedure** has been **methylene chloride** for a long time, and *the FDA has set a limit of 10 parts per million* for the leftover amounts in decaf coffee. Furthermore, methylene chloride levels routinely observed in independent coffee brand tests are within FDA guidelines. However, this chemical is also absorbed through the environment and is not limited to decaf coffee; therefore, it is a matter of conjecture how much of it anyone is absorbing during the day.

Humans are mainly exposed to methylene chloride **through inhalation**, which means that *contaminated air vapors* are most likely to cause exposure. Skin absorption is slow but may contribute to total body burden. Other than decaffeinated coffee, the main sources of this chemical include *paint strippers, aerosol sprays, and specific industrial processes, such as degreasing and pharmaceutical manufacturing*, where it is used as a solvent. Skin contact with contaminated materials can also cause exposure, but to a lesser degree.

How Much Caffeine Is in Your Drinks?

It has been found that adults can *safely consume up to 400 mg of caffeine daily.* Caffeine sensitivity, however, differs from person to person. You should probably cut back on coffee if it is giving you headaches, *irritability, or anxiety.* Anyone, but particularly pregnant women and those who may be sensitive to caffeine levels, should take into account the following assessments of caffeine levels in various beverages, according to research done by the Mayo Clinic.

The amount of caffeine in a cup of tea or coffee might vary greatly, so keep that in mind. And, caffeine content is affected by variables like processing and brewing duration. Here are the figures to help you out:

PRODUCT| OUNCES | CAFFEINE (mg.)

COFFEE DRINKS:

Brewed | 8 oz | 96

Brewed, decaf | 8 oz | 2

Espresso | 1 oz | 64

Espresso, decaf | 1 oz | 0

Instant | 8 oz | 62

Instant, decaf | 8 oz | 2

TEAS:

Brewed black | 8 oz | 47

Brewed black, decaf | 8 oz | 2

Brewed green | 8 oz | 28

Ready-to-drink | 8 oz | 19

SODAS:

Citrus (most) | 8 oz | 0

Cola | 8 oz (237) | 22

Root beer (most) | 8 oz | 0

ENERGY DRINKS:

Energy drink | 8 oz | 71.9

Energy shot | 2 oz | 215

Effects on Pregnant Women

NIH researchers found that daily coffee consumption during pregnancy is linked to **smaller babies**. For babies whose moms drank less than the 200 mg of caffeine daily (equivalent to around two cups of coffee), the researchers discovered that their size and lean body mass were correspondingly reduced. Babies who are born too small are more likely to develop health problems, including diabetes, obesity, and heart disease, as adults. But it's *not just caffeine consumption* that can lead to changes in utero during a baby's growth before birth.

High caffeine intake during pregnancy (over 200 mg daily) risks *fetal growth restriction*. While some research suggests that moderate caffeine consumption (200 mg or less per day) may be safe for pregnant women, other studies have shown conflicting findings. This has to be concerning for pregnant women, and if they are concerned, perhaps they should stay away from caffeinated beverages altogether.

Evidence for an increased risk of low birth weight and other adverse delivery outcomes *has been mixed*, with some studies finding a link and others finding none. Researchers in the NIH study pointed out that previous research *failed to take into consideration other variables* that can affect the size of the baby at birth, such as the fact that *various beverages have different caffeine contents* and that mothers smoke while they are pregnant. As is usual, many previously published studies have been found to be lacking in numerous variables that could have contributed to the present research results.

The Concern Regarding Coffee Decaffeination

The use of methylene chloride to remove caffeine from coffee is still controversial. Drinking decaf European method, like all coffee, may have some health benefits. Some research even points to coffee consumption as having heart benefits, but I'm not sure about the validity of that research and would advise caution here.

Many individuals who are switching to decaffeinated coffee are already at a higher risk of adverse reactions to trace substances, which is another concern. This group includes those who might switch to decaf for health reasons or while pregnant.

Major coffee businesses are responding to consumer concerns by using alternatives such as the Swiss water method more and more. Scientists believe green tea's active ingredient, EGCG, is responsible for its health benefits.

As with anything we consume, the bottom line is that everyone should be aware of what is in any product we are ingesting, whether it be a beverage or food. This responsibility may be difficult to apply to all food and beverage products because the information on the label does not contain all of the information we need. Your best hope is to research, especially if you have health concerns, and be an informed consumer—or as informed as possible.

Chapter 18: Food Is the Prescription, and Food Pharmacies Could Be the Way to Better Health

The world is full of health-hungry people, and it's not restricted to food but quality food that is healthy and protects us from deadly disorders and death. Food is not simply a means to sustain life and a pleasure we enjoy. It is an essential component of our health. Ignoring food's role in health denies its benefits and risks related to the lack of it. The current expression is not just implying that **food is**

a pharmaceutical (which it would appear to be) but that *prescribing food is a medical necessity*.

The long-term effects of COVID-19 are adding to the yearly death toll from diet-related chronic diseases in the US, which already stands at about one million. In the United States, malnutrition and chronic diseases such as type 2 diabetes, cardiovascular disease (CVD), obesity, and certain malignancies are **closely linked to poor dietary habits**, making them the **primary cause of death**.

Among individuals in the United States, about **40%** have pre-diabetes, and **11.3%** have diabetes; most of these instances are type 2 diabetes. Around **37%** of the U.S. population, or 126.9 million people aged 20 and more, will be living with cardiovascular disease in 2022. In 2021, there were **695,000** fatalities in the United States because of CVD, making it the top cause of death for both men and women.

Food Pharmacies

The food pharmacy is one new program model that aims to improve people's diets by *expanding their access to and consumption of healthy foods*, especially produce. According to the available studies on the food pharmacy model's effectiveness, these programs have helped patients better understand nutrition and overcome obstacles to healthy eating. As a result, they may have a major influence on health outcomes connected to diet.

Nevertheless, there has been a dearth of thorough research techniques and limited efforts to assess these programs' efficacy. To properly evaluate the long-term impacts of food pharmacy programs on healthy eating and diet-related health outcomes, additional study is required. But the current evidence provides more than food for thought on the topic. How is this concept implemented?

Therapeutic meals are meals specifically designed to meet medical needs, and the food as medicine initiative also includes prescriptions for healthy food, produce, and other foods. They are *usually supported by healthcare, the government, or charitable organizations*, administered by clinicians through the healthcare system, and patients pay nothing or very little for them. But these programs are limited to specific areas of the world.

Researchers identified 32 papers in the literature examining food as medicine interventions using a PubMed database search and by polling a network of international colleagues. Several instances were located in other Western countries, although the **majority were in the US**. Other countries that contributed were Canada, the UK, and Australia. *Brazil, Mexico, Germany, Ireland, and Finland did not have any*. Philanthropic funding, rather than institutional or organizational backing, was crucial for the majority of activities. Statistics on the health effects of food-as-medicine programs were inconsistently available in the scholarly literature, reflecting these endeavors' relative newness.

How Do They Work?

Located in Boston Medical Center! Founded in 2001, the Food Pantry dedicates itself to assisting low-income patients in overcoming nutrition-related illnesses and undernourishment. The food pantry serves as a bridge between patients and healthcare providers such as dietitians and doctors. Doctors at BMC clinics **provide food prescriptions** to improve patient health. Patients having *cancer, HIV/AIDS, high blood pressure, diabetes, obesity, cardiovascular disease*, and other long-term illnesses frequently visit the Pantry.

When it comes to nutrition, the goal of the food pharmacies at Children's Hospital of Philadelphia is to help families struggling to put food on the table. They strive to ensure that families have access to the food and financial resources they require by providing *direct grocery delivery* to their homes and offering one-on-one resource navigation. *Grocery delivery, financial consulting, and free fruit markets* are a few of the programs provided because of partnerships with local businesses and organizations. Families who sign up for the **Food Pharmacy program** get *free groceries for six months.*

Another program that integrates medicine and food is at TuftsUniversity. The Food Is Medicine launched at Tufts University's Friedman School of Nutrition Science and Policy. Its goal is to improve health care by implementing scalable food-based interventions. Interventions include *nutritional meals, doctor education, and improved clinical care for diet-related illnesses.*

The University of Utah Health's response to food insecurity is the Food Pharmacy program. This initiative is a component of the larger Driving Out Diabetes effort. In the late summer of 2020, the program was initially offered. Its goal is to help those in the community who are food insecure and dealing with long-term health issues related to nutrition. The food pharmacy *is a trailer* that can be moved and has all the necessary equipment for food service. Patients with a meal prescription from their clinician have access to a *large selection of nutritious food options* held by the pharmacy. Eligible individuals with valid referrals or prescriptions can pick up meals from the trailer at two sites during business hours.

The value of nutritious foods and meals **cannot be overstated** as we see the relationship between nutrition and disorders of physical and mentalhealth. In addition to providing healthful foods, these programs also encourage people to educate themselves regarding what they should eat; in addition, the programs, in the long run, can save government money on treating illnesses resulting from poor nutrition. One of the prime examples of these illnesses is **obesity worldwide**, which is of prime importance in health and medicine.

Chapter 19: Beans Are Now the Super Food That We All Need, So Get Ready for a New Diet

The lowly bean is finally receiving the accolades it deserves. Originally viewed as a diet staple of the poor, the bean is essential in more ways than previously thought, and research is indicating its value for everyone.

Higher scores for diet quality and greater consumption of shortfall nutrients, especially nutrients of public health concern, are associated with dietary patterns that are rich in canned and dry beans. Improved weight-related outcomes are also linked to bean dietary patterns. In essence, dietary recommendations for the United States should consider the nutritional and health advantages of encouraging more people to eat canned and dry beans.

But plant-based diets have some benefits that may surprise many. Reduced mortality from **prostate cancer** and improved ecological sustainability are only two of the several advantages of plant-based diets. According to a recent study conducted by academics, beans and peas are the most cost-effective and environmentally friendly alternatives to meat and milk. Given the current emphasis on environmental and climate change, we must consider alternatives to our current meat-based diet and assess their value. The study published in the PNAS found that soybeans, peas, and beans, as well as other legumes, **performed better than processed foods** like veggie burgers and plant milks.

Even after considering possible savings and investments, lab-grown meat was the **most ineffective substitute** due to its expensive price tag and the *absence of health advantages.*

What's This About "Pulses?"

Pulses have become less common in people's everyday diets, and the **prevalence of chronic diseases has increased** during the last century, both of which have altered people's eating patterns. Whole grain and legume consumption is associated with **improved cardiovascular, metabolic, and cognitive health** as well as **longer life expectancy**, according to dietary patterns. Contrarily, cardiovascular disease and premature death have been linked to diets heavy **in sugar, processed foods, and red meat.**

Some examples of *pulses* are peas, beans, and lentils. As an illustration, while pea pods are legumes, the **peas within them are the**

pulse. While most of us eat legumes for their seeds or pulses, the whole plant is used in agriculture for cover crops, cattle feed, and fertilizers. Pulses include beans of many varieties, including kidney, black, pinto, navy, chickpeas, and manymore. (This information was sourced from: https://nutritionsource.hsph.harvard.edu/legumes-p ulses/). But pulses aren't the only thing to consider. For example, beans are "resistant starches," and that is the importance they bring to our diet.

Everyday foods often contain starch, a type of carbohydrate. After cellulose, it is the chemical component of the chemicals in the highest abundance. In its chemical form, starch consists of two molecules of monosaccharide. Starch falls into one of three categories according to its physical and physiological characteristics: slowly digested or resistantstarch. It was also discovered that resistant starch *remained undigested,* and the gut microbial communities made use of these undigested carbohydrates. Here is where all the magic starts.

Resistant starch **does not raise blood sugar levels** since it is not broken down in the small intestine. Beneficial bacteria proliferate while harmful bacteria deplete as a result of fermentation in the large intestine, leading to an **improvement in gut health**. Glycemic management (especially important for diabetic patients) can be enhanced by promoting healthy gut bacteria. A *reduction in cholesterol levels and the danger of colon cancer* are among the other advantages of resistantstarch. It also helps with constipation and both treats and prevents it.Because of its long fermentation process, resistant starch produces less gas than other fiber types.

Our **best sources** of resistant starches include:

· Plantains and green bananas (as a banana ripens, the starch changes to regular starch)

· Beans, peas, and lentils (white beans and lentils are the highest in resistant starch)

· Whole grains, including oats and barley

· Cooked and cooled rice. Why "cooled" rice? Because it increases the resistant starch content.

So, beans aren't the only food with resistant starch qualities, but they are the easiest to obtain and least expensive when prepared in dried form. Canned beans may seem fine for quick meals, and that's true, but they also may contain high levels of salt, which is unsuitable for anyone's diet.

Concerned about your health and that of the plant? Reconsider a plant-based diet and beans as a staple in your meals. And, remember, ALWAYS check with your healthcare provider before any dietary changes you may want to make.

Chapter 20: One Spice (Cinnamon)That May Poison You or Kids

B aking and bread making have been found to be beneficial for our health, especially when it comes to kneading bread. Both have therapeutic effects, and the aroma of baked products in the home also adds to a sense of *calm and stress relief*. But in all of this, there may be an innocent introduction of a potentially dangerous space that all of us use frequently in baked goods—cinnamon. Why is cinnamon a potentially dangerous addition to our food and baked goods? The hidden danger in cinnamon is lead. It's not that anyone puts lead into the product, but it may be introduced in a variety of ways, including the manufacturing, storing, or some other form of processing the raw materials.

Lead is a metal that occurs naturally and is found in most foods. However, it can be harmful when consumed, particularly for young children and pregnant women. The CDC states that there is **no known "safe" level for lead contamination**. In light of the recent reports on cinnamon's potential heavy metal contamination, you may be asking whether it is safe to consume cinnamon or if you should just avoid it.

We should be concerned about the potential health risks, particularly for children, because *lead can damage the brain and other organs*. This contamination is likely due to environmental factors like **soil pollution, where** cinnamon trees are grown and **processing equipment is used** to grind the spice.

In 2024, research found that several brands of ground cinnamon contained concerning levels of lead. The FDA and Consumer Reports issued warnings as a result. According to the FDA's product testing results, the ground cinnamon items mentioned in their web table contain high levels of lead, which could be harmful if exposed to them for an extended period of time. Customers should not **purchase or use these ground cinnamon items,** as the FDA has recalled them. The Food and Drug Administration has asked the companies to remove these items from sale voluntarily. As more information from companies that have voluntarily agreed to a recall becomes available, the *FDA will update this warning* accordingly.

Why Lead Is Dangerous

Should lead in food be a cause for concern, considering its natural presence in soil and other potential sources? Undoubtedly, lead is not good for us, even though we may have some of it in our bodies.

Lead exposure poses **serious neurological risks to children and pregnant women**, potentially causing *developmental delays, learning difficulties, and behavioral problems*. On the other hand, adults are **not immune** to the side effects. Lead poisoning, for instance, has been associated with *lowered immunity, infertility, kidney disease, and high blood pressure.* But how does lead get into our bodies to cause these disturbing, damaging effects?

Lead is a dangerous metal that infiltrates our body *by masquerading as essential minerals* we need for healthy function. It primarily mimics two crucial elements—calcium and iron—which allows it to *sneak into our bloodstream and organs* undetected by our body's natural defense systems.

When lead enters our bloodstream, it begins a destructive process that impacts multiple body systems. Our blood cells unwittingly transport lead throughout the body, *reducing their capacity to carry essential iron.* This often results in **anemia**, where the body can't produce enough healthy red blood cells to function properly.

The most concerning damage occurs in our nervous system, particularly the brain. Lead interferes with normal brain function by *disrupting the calcium-dependent communication between neurons.* Like damaging the insulation on electrical wires, lead *deteriorates the protective myelin sheath around nerve fibers*, resulting in slower and confused signaling between brain cells.

Essential points about lead's dangerous nature:

• Lead **never breaks down in the body—and it accumulates** in the brain over time.

   • The body **stores lead in bones**, mistaking it for calcium

   • Children are particularly vulnerable to lead exposure

   • Even low-level exposure **can cause permanent damage**

What makes lead particularly dangerous is its *ability to store in bones* and release back into the bloodstream during times of stress or pregnancy. This means exposure can have effects long after the initial contact. The impact is especially severe in young children, whose *developing bodies absorb lead more readily* and whose growing brains are more susceptible to its toxic effects. This can result in *long-term learning difficulties, behavioral problems, and developmental delays.*

Lead mostly uses molecular mimicry to get into the body's transport systems; it mainly does this by **mimicking calcium** and, to a lesser degree, iron. Approximately 95% of the lead that enters the bloodstream binds to a protein known as delta-aminolevulinic acid dehydratase (ALAD), which enables lead to **adhere to red blood cells**. The binding process enables lead to enter the bloodstream and attach itself to cells that are normally responsible for transporting oxygen and nutrients.

In the blood-brain barrier, lead's calcium mimicking is especially sneaky. Although this barrier often prevents toxic compounds from entering the brain, lead manages to fool the gateway proteins into thinking it is calcium. Think of a lead **like a saboteur in a factory**—it doesn't just block work from happening; it *actively disrupts operations by pretending to be a worker* while damaging the machinery. This is why even small amounts of lead exposure over time can cause serious health problems, affecting learning, behavior, and overall development.

The Regulation of Lead in Cinnamon

Cinnamon and other spices are subject to FDA regulation, while heavy metals like lead are **not subject to any government limits**. The agency has the *option to track lead levels in spices* and notify the public when it detects an elevated level, either independently or in conjunction with a state. Heavy metal testing **remains infrequent in**

the United States. Asking questions and demanding transparency on social media might help alleviate concerns about the brands you use on a regular basis. To double-check, the Clean Label Project is another resource.

Consumers, who should be concerned about healthy foods and additives, are advised to check all websites that note recalls, pollution of products, or the presence of heavy metals in foods. This may not be a 100% solution to keeping yourself healthy, but it can add to your ability to know which ones to avoid and which ones may be questionable when you make purchases. We should also be aware that some individuals promote the use of cinnamon as a health-producing product that can have a variety of effects on the body. Again, please check with a qualified nutritionist or dietitian about this before engaging in any type of supplemental use of cinnamon in your diet.

Chapter 21: Cancer Gets Its Start in Our Mouths, Stressing Oral Care More Than Ever

B rushing your teeth and regular visits to your dental hygienist should be high on your list of preventive care when it comes to cancer and Alzheimer's disease/dementia. Alterations to the oral microbiome raise the risk of disease, but a balanced microbiota helps avoid cancer.

One study indicated that the risk of stomach cancer is 52% higher in persons who have a history of gum disease. People with over a dozen types of bacteria in their mouths are 50% more likely to develop head and neck squamous cell carcinoma. Dental care, in the simplest terms, is vital if you want to remain as disease-free as possible. It's not a guarantee, but look at the statistics. Our perspective on dental hygiene needs to be adjusted. More and more, research is coming to the conclusion that taking care of it could be the hidden key to a longer and better life.

A healthy oral microbiome, which includes the 700 or so species of bacteria, fungi, and viruses that call our mouths home, is more important than perfect teeth in and of itself. Neglecting our dental hygiene can lead to systemic infections that are worse or cause conditions including arthritis, cancer, heart disease, and Alzheimer's.

When did we ever think that Alzheimer's might get its foothold in our brains via our mouths? This certainly adds to the current belief that this type of dementia is caused by a certain type of amyloid in the brain. Do these amyloid plaques begin via viruses or other bacteria in the mouth? There is a good possibility that this connection may be vital to maintaining our cognitive health.

Mouth to Body to Brain

The oral germs that cause gum disease can spread to the bloodstream. Bacteria in this stage invade your blood vessel walls and secrete a class of chemicals known as cytokines. Arteries supplying the heart and brain can be damaged by systemic inflammation caused by these substances, leading to a higher risk of cardiovascular events. Experts also believe that the nervous system may be affected by inflammation, which could cause mental health disorders like depression and anxiety.

An emergency medical response is necessary in the case of brain swelling. If left untreated, brain swelling from an untreated tooth infection can manifest as a variety of symptoms, including vomiting, nausea, headaches, and confusion. A tooth infection is not a simple infection, as research has shown, and can lead to extremely serious damage to various parts of the body and brain. When we consider this connection, it becomes eminently clear that health insurance should cover dental care because of its vital connection to overall health.

Even sinus drainage may be necessary to alleviate pressure on the brain in patients with severe tooth infections or abscesses, which are pockets in the gums filled with pus. Rarely, if not treated promptly, a ruptured abscess near the ear or eye socket might cause lasting damage to an artery.

Recent research has shown the role of the oral microbiota in the development of colorectal and stomach cancers. Researchers observed that the risk of stomach cancer increased by 33% in individuals who had lost two or more teeth and by 52% in those with a history of gum disease compared to those without gum disease. Polyps, which can progress to colon cancer, are more common in patients with gum disease (17% higher risk compared to healthy individuals) and in those without gum disease. According to the research, patients with a history of four or more tooth extractions were also 20% more likely to develop these polyps.

Do You Know How to Maintain Your Dental Health?

One obvious answer is to visit your dentist at least once a year and your dental hygienist possibly twice a year. This will ensure that any incipient problems will be quickly discovered, and appropriate action taken to remediate it.

How many times a day should we brush our teeth, as well as how (the direction in which we should brush) to brush, and what should we use to maintain good oral hygiene? Numerous products are on the market in terms of both manual and electronic toothbrushes as well as flossers and gum irrigators that flush below the gum to remove debris. But which is best and which should be avoided are two questions that deserve answers.

Know what the American Dental Association recommends regarding oral health and maintaining your teeth? Here are their suggestions:

1. Twice daily, brush your teeth. For two minutes per session, brush your teeth using a toothbrush with soft bristles and fluoride toothpaste. If you want to keep cavities, gum recession, and periodontitis at bay, brush your teeth at least twice a day.

2. Just remember to floss once a day Flossing is an effective alternative to brushing for cleaning in between teeth, where toothbrush bristles can not reach.

3. If you want to whiten your teeth, freshen your breath, and minimize plaque and gingivitis, then you should use mouthwash. NOTE: Not all mouthwash products contain alcohol, and they indicate this prominently on the label. Check first before you make a purchase.

4. Both children and adults should see a dentist twice a year for professional teeth cleaning.

5. Invest in a new toothbrush. Every three to four months, change the head on your electric toothbrush or manual toothbrush.

6. Pick the correct method. Use light, back-and-forth strokes while holding the toothbrush at a 45-degree angle to the gum line. Use a vertically angled brush and up-and-down strokes to clean the inner surfaces of your front teeth.

7. Put dental picks or interdental brushes to use. Use these instruments to floss in between your teeth if you are short on dexterity.

8. Go for gum that does not include any sugar. While sugar-free gum can aid in cavity prevention, it should not be used in place of regular brushing and flossing.

Good oral hygiene can go a long way to maintaining and improving your physical health, and now, with the new connection to cancer, it's more important than ever.

Chapter Twenty-Two

Chapter 22: Reward Time Is Here and We Need to Know What to Do to Help Ourselves

I n terms of impact, negative experiences outweigh positive ones in the following contexts: daily life, big life events (such as trauma), the results of intimate relationships, patterns in social networks, interactions between individuals, and the learning process. **We give greater weight to negative feelings**, parents, and criticism than positive ones, and we give more weight to negative information while processing it than positive. What can we do about it?

Many people now consider happiness to be the most important thing in life, and there has been a dramatic increase in the public's interest in the subject in recentdecades. With more and more people interested in finding pleasure, scientists have been eager to determine if this trend has any positive effect on health. It seems to reason that individuals will attract more happiness into their lives if they make it a priority to be happy.

One study examined 8,331 Dutch people as part of the Longitudinal Internet Studies for the Social Sciences (LISS) panel. Beginning in 2019 and continuing through 2023, the poll asked participants to rate their own happiness and several other well-being markers, such as life satisfaction, positive and negative emotions, and the strength of their relationships.

According to the research, those *whose happiness was more highly valued were more likely to be happy overall*. In particular, those *who prioritized pleasure had fewer negative emotions,* more frequent pleasant ones, and better overall levels of life satisfaction. These results are in line with the theory that **people can improve their level of contentment and happiness** in their daily lives by making happiness a life goal. No one is suggesting that you should walk around being happy all the time because a variety of mood states is normal and denying that could mean there is an underlying problem that is not being addressed.

The Happiness Route

There are a number of things that can help us through the roughest of times and regain some of the happiness we seek. Here are a few:

1. One method by which people gain personal and social resources while also savoring positive experiences is by sharing them with others.

Previous studies have proven that this process, known as capitalization, has significant advantages even in the physical health of patients with cancer.

2. Let happiness be the ultimate aim, not the means to an end. If you want to live a better life, *prioritize good, proven activities like exercising, spending time with loved ones or friends, or being outside in nature.* We have a trove of research that points to being in nature, utilizing forest therapy, and exercising as all proven to have enormous benefits in our physical and mental health. Exercising has now been shown to **increase brain connections** and the neurons that flourish to keep us cognitively aware and functioning.

3. Make a list of three to five bullet points detailing all that you are thankful for that day before turning in for the night. Things and people that you are thankful for on any given day are not major life events but rather ordinary occurrences.

4. Keep an optimistic outlook and look for the best in others. The truth is that there are darker sides to life than rainbows and unicorns. Never take the people or things that bring us joy for granted; instead, learn to embrace and cope with everything life throws at us. Everything should be treasured since we never know when it will all be gone.

5. Feel the anger and let it out. Just hold on for a second before you go on. Alternatively, if you are short on time, get over it and deal with your disappointment later.

6. Try out this website for some free inspiration and happiness tools that havebeen created by an educational psychologist: articulatingyo urstrengths.org

7. Find and maintain a purpose in life that provides you with a sense offulfillment. Without purpose, we can become victims of ourselves; therefore, it is within our grasp—just find it and hang on.

As one 90-something man told a residential housing worker, life is a roller coaster, and you must learn to ride the waves. No one expects you to be a Pollyanna, nor should you be Chief Rain-in-the-Face. So, go forth and prosper. Member, you're not a comic book character, but someone who will experience many emotions – some of them upsetting, but some also being comforting.

Chapter Twenty-Three

Chapter 23: Science Is Now Studying Outrage

• The Internet is proving to be a wonderful resource for researchers seeking a wide range of subjects. One area being explored includes the science of outrage. What drives outrage, and can certain platforms use it to their financial advantage? This new database of subjects speeds up research and sparks future initiatives. Therefore, it is a welcomed addition to our research methodology; however, with any research, issues always need to be resolved in future efforts.

Nothing is pristine or perfect, and we need to keep that in mind. As Aristotle knew, we are inherently imperfect and live in an imperfect world. For example, one of my professors once challenged the class to draw a perfect circle. After that, he indicated that there is no such thing as a perfect circle—that exists in a perfect world where we don't exist.

In our imperfection, rage is endemic to human behavior, but it has both positive and negative effects. Even though most people would rather not deal with it, it has some "good" aspects, such as making individuals more optimistic, less risk-averse, and more motivated to confront obstacles.

Anger, a key feeling in outrage, in particular, motivates people to take aggressive action, meaning they want to fight back against whatever is making them angry. As a result, anger significantly impacts the willingness to punish criminals and restore justice. Faced with policies contradicting one's ideology, outrage can motivate political action.

In a recent study, researchers randomly assigned more than half a million Facebook users to one of five political parties to observe how each group's members reacted. Research shows users are inclined to interact with posts that oppose their opinions, especially when their core beliefs are in question. According to the researchers, some social media sites and users use people's wrath to boost participation. Any kind of user engagement, favorable or negative, is good for the platform. Do platforms, then, skew the content to achieve that goal? There must always be this one question regarding any material, whether or not it's an Internet platform.

Additionally, the study discovered that engagement is not a reliable measure of consumer preferences. Political engagement originates from anger, in contrast to participation in other areas, such as fashion or sports, demonstrating interest. This can lead to a vicious cycle.

The Internet and Responses

With matters of fundamental principles or deeply held views, people seek out information that confirms their existing opinions and shun information that contradicts them. Examining social media posts on controversial topics uncovers a more complex pattern, challenging congeniality bias. Increasingly, individuals with opposing ideological beliefs dominate or even influence online discussions, where negative sentiments are often expressed.

Research from Tulane University sheds light on why people who strongly disagree with something are more likely to engage with it. The researchers identified a phenomenon known as the "confrontation effect." This means that individuals are more prone to engage with content that questions their beliefs rather than stuff that supports them.

Users commonly respond to opposing ideas with increased participation, often motivated by anger, according to the study's analysis of data from online experiments, Twitter, and Facebook over time, including the 2020 US presidential election. The study sheds light on the numerous instances of harmful rhetoric that we encounter on the internet. According to the findings, those who use harmful rhetoric are highly motivated to express their anger against those they disagree with.

Situations that cause negative thoughts regarding the acts or characters of others trigger a range of emotions known as "other-condemning experiences" in people. Situations that are personally insulting, obstruct goal-directed activities or reveal an unfairness or malicious purpose (particularly when another person is held responsible) are all potential triggers for anger.

People usually take it easy after making a mistake [post-error slowdown, or PES). While formerly thought to indicate adaptive, regulated processing, newer research doubts this idea. It proposes that error processing is an unintended consequence of the unexpected character of errors.

Neuroimaging studies suggest the brain may have a specialized mechanism for handling errors. But does it? If it does, where do facts and reason come into play, or are they seen as distorted and false? How ingrained are negative beliefs when infused with high emotion? What part might the emotional part of the brain, the amygdala, play?

Our rational thinking parts of the brain are susceptible to hijacking by the amygdala. Common emotional triggers include anger, hostility, fear, and stress. Their effects might be abrupt, unreasonable, and even absurd.

But what part does the Internet play in all of this? Nowadays, it is hard to find a place to talk about politics and morality without mentioning online social networks. Psychologists have not yet determined the factors that contribute to the disproportionate dissemination of certain political and moral ideologies.

Social media analysis shows moral-emotional language works well for group messaging but not for contentious policy issues like gun control. These results provide insights into the transmission of moral concepts within networks during actual political discourse.

Both the value of social network approaches to the study of morality and the role of emotions in the transmission of moral ideas within social groups are important. Research results shed light on how people's social networks expose them to moral and political beliefs that can inform new theories of social influence and group polarization.

It is incorrect to assume that people only use the Internet in a negative way because it is a valuable tool for idea dissemination and discussion. However, the manner in which this discourse takes place is of prime consideration. When information is specifically and intentionally distorted, we must call it out in terms of research and the common good.

Chapter 24: What's a Psychiatrist, and What's a Psychologist?

A friend recently told me he had to change his therapist because the therapist was going to a new job. He had no choice in who would be his next therapist at that institution, which, might I say, is an enormous place, but he assumed it would work out smoothly. His assumption, unfortunately, was premature.

At this first therapy appointment, the woman behind the desk asked about his health and medication. After about 15 to 20 minutes, she indicated that they would have another appointment in 2 months. He was more than shocked and amazed since he had been seen weekly for therapy sessions.

When he asked the young woman, *"But you are my therapist, correct?"* She responded in a nonplussed manner, *"No, I am a psychiatrist, and I don't do therapy."* So, he had not been seeing a psychiatrist? Clearly, he hadn't, and he had been seeing either a psychology intern or a social work intern—information that nobody had ever given to him. He just assumed something that was patently incorrect.

The world of mental health has undergone seismic changes in the last 30 years or even more. Originally, psychiatrists went through a period of psychoanalytic training, which was the norm. Once biopsychiatry began to make its place in the world of healthcare and **backed up its conclusions with hard data rather than dream analysis**, training programs dropped psychoanalysis altogether.

I can remember being at a large hospital in a major East Coast setting, where a young psychiatrist in training felt abandoned. His program was no longer continuing his psychoanalytic training but biopsychotherapy instead. He was well into his training and didn't know what he was going to do. At that point in his career, he felt that his work would always include psychoanalysis, but now it wouldn't. I never discovered how he resolved his dilemma, but I imagine he had to transition to biopsychatry and abandon psychoanalytic training or leave the program, and who leaves a residency in the middle of a program?.

Anyone wishing for a bit more background, or should I say *backstory of psychoanalysis*, should read "The Assault on Truth," "Freud and His Followers," and "Mind Fixers: Psychiatry's Troubled Search for the Biology of Mental Illness." I would also suggest reading one of Freud's works, "Moses & Monotheism." Or, for a truly different perspective, read "The Myth of Mental Illness" by Thomas Szasz.

The Testing Divide

Nowhere in their training are psychiatrists trained to administer psychological tests other than the brief checkmark forms developed by pharmaceutical companies for their research protocols. Personally, I have had an interaction that pointed out how this can affect a psychiatrist's work.

While working at a facility as a consulting psychologist and being paid far less than psychiatrists who were doing the same work as I, a psychiatrist came over to me and *asked me to interpret psychological testing* that had been given to him and on which he was to write a report.

He had no idea how to do an IQ test or what each of its scales would indicate about an individual. In truth, he was asking for a mini-seminar that could not possibly provide him with the information he would've gotten had he been trained in psychological testing. I couldn't make up for that lack, but I tried to give him a quick overview, and I assume he used that in everything that he evaluated in the future. For me, I didn't think he had sufficient training or experience for the reports and people's benefits were based on his reports. It was an ethical conundrum.

Medicine, Psychiatry and Psychology

Separating both the physical and the mental into two different areas, to me and too many other people, doesn't make much sense. They both work in concert, and all of us need to be familiar with everything. We cannot seclude ourselves in our own little area of one profession. I can remember when a *psychologist asked me for information on Xanax* because one of her patients, who had an alcohol problem, was taking it.

I expressed serious concern since I knew that Xanax (a benzodiazepine) is a potentiator when used with alcohol and can be quite dangerous. She had no idea because *she had almost no training in biology* and knew nothing about psychiatric medications.

I wondered how she could consider herself *working in an ethical manner* if she didn't increase that knowledge now that I had brought it to her attention. This was an individual who had at least **five or six brass plaques on her door**, indicating that she had additional training in specific areas of therapy. In a word, ego was stronger than ethics.

The healthcare situation has become a bit more muddled for some because *MDs are no longer the only specialists in healthcare permitted to prescribe.* Now, **nurse practitioners and psychologists** who have taken specific courses to obtain pharmaceutical licensing privileges can write prescriptions. States may have particular requirements for other-than-MDs to prescribe, and anyone wishing for more information is advised to go to their local state's website to do further research on this.

Chapter 25: Forever Chemicals and Microplastics in Water More Dangerous to Health Than Thought

T he refreshing glass of cold water from your home, school, or work tap may hold *dangers you have never envisioned*. Once you understand the current state of PFAS entrance into the system, you may never again be as casual about your water consumption.

We already know about the microplastics that have been found everywhere, including the rivers, lakes, deep oceans, and our bodies' blood. It is inescapable at this time, but the PFAS chemicals may be something that can be controlled in some manner.

For anyone continuing to use bottled water in the belief that it is safer than water from your tap, there is research that can be a bit unsettling. A liter of bottled water had an average of 240,000 microplastic particles, with over 90% of those particles being nanoplastics, according to astudy. Previous research had largely concentrated on bigger microplastics; therefore, this amount represented a **tenfold to one hundredfold increase**.

The potential damage has been ongoing for the last half century or so. Some of the health damage begins through our constant dependence on plastics—that miracle" product of the 1940s that has become so entrenched in our lives that we can't seem to exist without it. Discarded and broken down consumer goods, such as single-use plastic bottles, food packaging, and plastic pellets—tiny bits of plastic utilized to create packaging, automotive components, toys, and other things—give rise to microplastics, which are defined as fragments of plastic shorter than 5 millimeters in length.

Microplastics *end up in human water sources* because of ocean dumping and landfills. These bits also *make it into the air* when plastic-filled bubbles burst at the surface of the ocean, according to the World Health Organization, and into lakes, rivers, and estuaries. They have even found microplastics in the breath of dolphins. And microplastics may also bring on climate change, as we are now discovering. Clouds may form in environments where they would not generally due to microplastics in the air, which could have an impact on the weather and climate.

Additionally, humans can consume microplastics more directly, **most frequently through food**. For example, a study conducted in Italy found *plastics in fish* meant for human consumption, while scientists in China discovered thousands of tons of microplastics on *farmland and in crops*. Another study found that containers, especially those subjected to high temperatures, can *leach microplastics into the food they contain*.

Have you ever considered that your *disposable container or cup* might be filling your food or drink with dangerous plastic or chemicals? Most of us would never have had that thought, **but now we cannot escape it.** Each sip and each bit of food is another opportunity on a journey toward illness.

In this age of prioritizing health, we have complete control over this area without needing a gym or exercise. All we need to do is to try to eliminate certain items from our lives. While you're at it, consider all those non-stick cooking utensils you use and research them and what they might put into your body. Would you rather have material that wasn't so resistant to sticking and save your health in the process? Of course, this is a rhetorical question because we all want to remain healthy for as long as possible.

What PFAS Chemicals Do

PFAS has been used in various products since the 1950s because they *effectively repel water and grease.* Water, soil, plants, sludge, serum from humans and animals, and tissues are just some of the matrices where they have been found, attesting to their environmental durability. But in addition to their ability to withstand adverse environmental conditions, they remain **serious neurotoxins**. These toxic chemicals have even been found in menstrual pads and may contribute to reproductive issues in the future

The National Health and Nutrition Examination Survey, an initiative run by the CDC in the United States, reports that the typical American has a blood level of about 4.7 ppb.

And it doesn't end there. A number of major health issues have been linked to exposure to high amounts of PFAS, according to studies. These include *cancer, liver and immune system damage, developmental effects on fetuses during pregnancy or on breastfed infants, thyroid issues, and high cholesterol.*

Researchers now believe that poor gut health, brought on by harmful PFAS forever chemical exposure in young adults, contributes to kidney illness in the future. A recent 2024 study has now opened up new concerns. More than two years after a Maine dairy farmer and his wife stopped drinking the milk and water from their farm, blood tests on both showed levels of the "forever chemicals" **20 times the national average.**

The family doctor had submitted blood tests for them to a lab. There was 111 ppb **of PFAS** in his blood and **93.5 ppb in his wife.** *A blood level of about 4.7 ppb is typical for Americans.* What caused this? The farm used *contaminated sludge* **from a paper factory.**

One example of how this sludge may get into our water system and air is illustrated by an investigation in Florida where sludge is used in a variety of ways. According to the Florida DEP, over 40 facilities produce an estimated 350,000 tons of biosolids. Of that, 100,000 dry tons go straight to landfills. On land, another 100,000 are dispersed.

About 200,000 tons of biosolid "fertilizer" is made from the remaining 150,000 dry **tons by mixing and mulching it with landscape material.** How safe is fertilizer in the rest of the states that might be producing similar products from sludge? It might be an interesting area to explore wherever you may live and buy fertilizer.

Various health problems like **cancer, liver damage, and developmental issues** can occur at high levels. When we see blood results like this, we cannot overstate the danger of PFAS. It might lead us to wonder if we should have our blood tested and what the result would be if we were to test. This is not to say that everyone needs to run out and have a blood test for PFAS, but if there is concern about certain serious and/or neurologic disorders, perhaps this would be indicated as a rule-out possibility.

I once evaluated a young man whose wife complained that he was having severe bouts of depression, rages, and sleep problems. Once I delved into his lifestyle, I discovered he was a landscaper and frequently used a variety of pesticides and fertilizers. He was, of course, then referred for further evaluation by a neurologist and a hematologist. He had elevated levels of chemicals in his blood, and his "mental disorder" was the result of close, daily interaction with these materials, where he both inhaled and had these products on his skin. Not long ago, a friend's husband, a horticulturist for a major corporation's extensive grounds, died of cancer and I can only suspect it was from the fertilizer and pesticides he used for his landscaping job.

What Can You Do to Protect Yourself?

The Environmental Protection Agency recommends that if you have questions about your household drinking water, whether it comes from the town water supply or private wells, you might want to have the water tested. When purchasing items that are indicated to be water-resistant *or have some other form of protection*, that protection may contain PFAS. It is, therefore, on the consumer's part that each individual can make changes in their life. It's not easy, but isn't your health worth it?

Certain PFAS may still be present in indoor air or dust, even if there have been recent attempts to remove them from commerce, reducing the probability of exposure. Call (301) 504–8120 or email ConsumerOmbudsman@cpsc.gov to reach the Consumer Ombudsman, who is part of the Consumer Product SafetyCommission. You can also visit their website.

Technology has made wonderful advances and has improved our lives, but some of the changes may not be as beneficial as we had hoped. As before, each of us must remember that phrase "**caveat emptor,**" "**let the buyer beware.**" It's always good advice.

Chapter 26: Kids, X-Rays, CAT Scans, and Cancer, Oh, My!

The monthly medical meeting was uneventful, with the usual information being dispensed under department regulations. All the healthcare providers waited for it to be over until one pediatrician stood up to tell the group something that troubled him.

"The other day, a mother and her child came into my office," he said, *"and she praised the local clinic where her child had been receiving treatment. She said they were so good and so careful that each time she brought her child in, **they took an x-ray of his body.**"* This might have happened several times a year.

The physician turned and looked at the group, waiting for some response. There was none, and it seemed perfectly fine with everyone that *this child was repeatedly being exposed to needless X-rays*. It was an example of disregard for ethical norms or medical needs, especially with children.

Questions must be raised, and adequate answers must be given when any type of radiation is necessary for the detection or treatment of specific illnesses or diagnoses. Viewing this in any other way should be discouraged because patients have a right to know of any dangers or benefits that will accrue to them. Is this the case every time? Obviously, that was not the case in the illustration of the parent-physician interaction above. Patients also must wonder *how many of these procedures in a year would be safe* for them, and that's a **reasonable request**, too. No one wants their child to develop cancer, and excessive exposure to radiation may be one cause.

Ionizing radiation, which includes high-energy wavelengths or particles, is used in x-ray, computed tomography (CT), and nuclear imaging. This type of radiation can penetrate tissue and show the inside organs and structures of the body. Despite your cells' best efforts, ionizing *radiation can damage DNA*. However, even their repairs are not always complete, and there may be small patches of "misrepair." This causes DNA alterations, which can increase the risk of cancer in the future.

Pediatric Use and Risk

Among imaging modalities, computed tomography (CT) produces the highest radiation *exposures*, yet it is an effective diagnostic tool. Radiation shielding is crucial, especially for youngsters. One study looked at the possibility of brain tumors and leukemia in children exposed to low doses of ionizing radiation from CT scans.

The study concluded that exposure to radiation from CT scans increased the incidence of **brain tumors** in a retrospective *cohort of 168,394 children* in the Netherlands. Regarding leukemia, no correlation (i.e., no cause and effect) was found. It is important to exercise caution when interpreting the results because the sample of *children who had CT scans displayed a higher incidence of brain tumors* compared to the overall population. It was possibly a misrepresentative sample, but it could provide some evidence for additional caution with children.

In addition, patients who have computed tomographic (CT) scans before the age of 22 may be at a higher risk of developing blood malignancies. Research using data from about 900,000 youngsters in Europe who had at least one scan revealed an almost two fold increased excess risk per 100 mGy dosage.

At an average dose of 8 mGy per scan, these **results imply that 1 to 2 children per 10,000** who get CT scans are likely to acquire a blood malignancy such as **non-Hodgkin lymphoma or acute leukemia** *because of radiation.*

In a European study, lower but still elevated risk estimates were obtained, especially for lymphoid malignancies, where the number of cases was lowered when the period of *follow-up was limited to 2 years* following the maximum age at first CT in each nation.

As indicated by other studies, concern remains. Despite the benefits, medical professionals are worried about cancer risk and reduced pediatric CTs due to high cumulative doses.

Adult Risk Considered

There were a total of twenty-five studies that utilized 111,649,943 participants, with a mean age of 45.37 years and an *83.4% female representation.* Out of these, 2,049,943 were participants from six studies with participants ranging from 5 to 80 years. Following CT scans, the risk of cancer in adults was significantly elevated. **Radiation exposure and the number of CT scan locations** both raise the likelihood of cancer.

Study quality and time phrases were not significantly different from one study to another, nor were gender, age, nation, or continent. Were females more at risk, or did they receive more radiation through CT scans?

However, changes have come to the CT scan and radiation received by patients. Although CT scans pose little risk to patients, they expose them to small amounts of radiation. Patients subjected to higher radiation doses are **those who require more frequent scans** to track their health or who undergo specialist CT exams, such as CT perfusion (CTP).

Radiologists have a delicate balancing act to accomplish when deciding on a course of treatment: use a larger dose to acquire better quality images for diagnosis or a lower dose to get lower quality images. Now, AI has entered healthcare, and it is making a difference in CT scans.

CT scans continue to be an important diagnostic and treatment device, but healthcare professionals should use them only when there is a specific need and minimize the number of scans required. Research also shows that those with **specific diseases** may require more frequent scans and accumulate more radiation exposure during their lifetime (LAR).

Chapter 27: Dying of Medical Disbelief Shouldn't Happen

A t 27 years of age, Maeve Boothby O'Neill should not have died because of ill-conceived, poorly managed medical studies and, ultimately, **medical ignorance**. She was a victim no less than anyone else who has been dismissed, disbelieved, improperly diagnosed, and inappropriately treated to where death was inevitable. We should not overlook her death and should use it as a guiding light to **pierce the web of disbelief** created by those who refuse to entertain doubts.

Her illness? It was **myalgic encephalomyelitis/chronic fatigue syndrome (ME/CFS).**

How did it happen, and is it happening to too many others, not just in the UK, but worldwide? Medical literature is supposed to guide us, inform us, and help us to maintain patients' health as best we can. In healthcare, there may not always be apparent charlatans but *poorly planned studies* and *misguided beliefs about psychological illness.* Quality assurance committees are also responsible.

I would refer anyone who wants to keep up on the *retractions of fraudulent or improperly concocted science* to one place on the Internet—**Retraction Watch.** The latest shocking revelation in this online publication involves a cancer researcher who used **manipulated images** in several papers. Although he has had numerous publications retracted now, he still maintains his position at a highly respected hospital in a major city in the United States. Unfortunately, *he is not alone in this practice*, but we are fortunate to have those willing to ferret them out. Even the famed Karolinska Institute has had its issues.

What Is ME/CFS?

The debilitating effects of myalgic encephalomyelitis and chronic fatigue syndrome (ME/CFS) prevent sufferers from leading their regular lives. It hinders both mental and physical exertion. Difficulty concentrating, extreme fatigue, and other symptoms may be present. Neither a cause nor a remedy has been found. Addressing the most pressing symptoms is common practice when providing care. But what therapy, when, and for how long, especially if we don't know what causes it?

Limited access to healthcare may contribute to the underdiagnosis of ME/CFS. Additionally, we may require *more medical professionals who are familiar with ME/CFS* and capable of identifying the symptoms.

A new blood test could differentiate between patients with ME/CFS and healthy people or disease controls with an **impressive 91% accuracy rate**. How many facilities or healthcare professionals are using it?

Unfortunately, they placed *too much emphasis on psychological causes* and referred patients for this type of therapy. Negative attitudes toward patients who were upset about their inability to get symptom relief were rife.

How many times have MS patients (usually women) been seen as "attention-seeking" or "noncompliant" or labeled with other terms that failed to help and made their lives more miserable? I knew of a woman with MS that the *family therapist castigated* and engaged the family in viewing her as *unwilling to get well.* Once the diagnosis was established, I never heard how the therapist addressed the damage done to the woman's self-esteem.

How Has the Stigma Been Addressed?

The damage has been done to more patients than we know. Only the case of Ms. O'Neill has *risen to the attention of the popular press* in the UK. What of the others that may have been missed and not picked up?

Following Ms. O'Neill's revealing autopsy report in the UK, new guidelines have been established by the National Institute for Health and Care Excellence in response to the young woman's tragic death. They **rescinded their previous guidelines** and set out new ones based on their findings of *poor methodology of studies, debunked theories, and inadequate care*. Their aim? The prevention of future deaths.

The new guidelines expressly indicate that healthcare professionals not prescribe:

1. an exercise- or movement-based treatment for chronic fatigue syndrome

2. exercise or physical activity programs for all age groups, including those with and without specific medical conditions

3. a regimen like graded exercise therapy (GET) that involves pre-determined progressive increases in physical activity or exercise

4. sustaining physical activity or exercise programs that are grounded in the theories of deconditioning and exercise intolerance

Would Ms. O'Neill be alive and participating in the normal lifestyle of a 27-year-old woman if her team/teams had adhered to these guidelines? We'll never know because *years of disregard had done the damage*. Were the metaphors of her symptoms not understood, or were existing theoretical myths **of the origin of her illness** stronger than common sense?

The new guidelines state that healthcare professionals should "recognize *that people with ME/CFS may have experienced **prejudice and disbelief** and could **feel stigmatized** by people (including family, friends, health and social care professionals, and teachers) **who do not understand their illness**.*"

It's more than unfortunate that change only comes about in healthcare, methodology and diagnosing when tragedy, such as a death, strikes. We can only equate it with neighborhoods that have traffic lights installed after someone is killed by a car speeding through an intersection.

It will not bring that person back, and it illustrates that we should not have to wait for that type of tragedy to occur in order for change to occur. Where is the change that we need now, and in what illnesses or disorders? **That is the question that must be posed by researchers in all fields of medical endeavor.**

Chapter 28: Dancing or Watching Stimulates Your Brain — All Good

We've all read the stories before, and we marvel at them because they tell of the old, old seniors who are enjoying life to the fullest, and one of their activities is **dancing**. Yes, the simple activity that anyone can do, whether alone, with a partner, or in a group, is now **being given the recognition it deserves.**

How many times have you heard a reporter ask a 100-year-old person for their secrets to a long life? And what do they usually say is one activity that keeps them going? *Dancing is right up there with community activities,* religious affiliation, and family love.

Researchers are also seeking the answer that we all crave, and now professional publications are starting to make their results available to all of us. Few people would have to be told that exercise is one of the best ways to maintain your physical and mental health because *muscles do more than work like rubber bands, holding our bones and joints together.* Muscles serve as *workhorses for other biochemical reactions,* and we still haven't completely unraveled the mystery of muscles.

Dancing is a muscle-activating means of not simply moving around and exercising but also *soothing and activating our brains.* Before studying the intricate mental coordination needed for dance, scientists *paid little attention to the neurological impact of dancing.*

According to neuroscientists, a "**pleasure double play**" occurs when bodies move in time with music. Neuroscientists explain that music activates the *brain's reward areas,* whereas dance activates the *sensory and motor circuits.*

Researchers have used positron emission tomography (PET) scans to pinpoint specific brain **areas involved in dancing**. The motor cortex facilitates all three stages of voluntary movement—**preparation, regulation, and execution.** There is sufficient evidence now that *dancing has physical benefits similar to exercise,* **including better memory and stronger connections between neurons**. Such a simple thing to do, i.e., dancing, and yet so powerful.

Where would dance therapy be most effective if not specifically aimed at mood disorders? With an estimated prevalence of 1% among those aged 60 and up, Parkinson's disease (PD) is the *second most common neurological illness worldwide.* It has complicated clinical manifestations and is a systemic disease. Non-motor symptoms, including mood disorders, sleep disturbances, cognitive and sensory dysfunctions, and motor symptoms, can result from neuronal loss and neurotransmitter imbalances.

Patients with Parkinson's are now receiving **dance therapy** as part of their treatment plans. Why would that be? Dancing is an exercise that engages more than just your muscles; it *also engages your brain, emotions, social circle, and senses.*

Dancing helps people with PD with their motor skills, which are impaired due to neuromuscular demands, including *mobility, balance, coordination, and direction changes,* as well as other motor capacities like *endurance, flexibility, and strength.* It may seem counterintuitive to some, but dancing is one way to help anyone with Parkinson's *begin to regain some of the skills that need help.*

What Types of Dancing?

Too many people believe that dancing *adheres to a specific formula of footsteps and body movements,* and that is simply not the case. Dancing is movement that brings freedom and a sense of joy from the freedom to move to the music however you wish. A listing of potential dances is mind-boggling, and anyone can find something to suit their needs.

Are there specific types of dancing that might be more helpful than others? This is open to consideration, and the easiest and simplest answer is **whatever pleases you**. You may want to *dance with a partner or learn an intricate step for a dance* that is no longer seen, such as the *Paso Doble* or something more in step with what is known as line dancing or the two-step, or even the Electric Slide. But there's more here that needs to be considered, and the one word we need to keep in mind is "freedom." Haven't you ever felt the need to move around without restriction to the steps that must be followed? Dance is what you wanted to be and it can be whatever you want—twirling, dipping, taking small jumps—whatever.

A new health study found that most people with a *history of trauma, sadness, or anxiety* saw improvements in their mental health after participating in conscious dancing. This activity promotes self-discovery via **unchoreographed movement.** It's dancing that is helpful for those with mental health issues, as well as for managing regular stress, particularly in older individuals. **Dance as you wish** would seem to be the instruction here.

Even folk dancing has its place in therapeutic activities. A study tested a **modified folk-dance intervention** in **at-risk youth** to enhance their emotional and physical health and overall quality of life. Based on the major findings, the customized folk dance improved mental and physical fitness. Based on the findings of the pre- and post-tests for mental health, the customized folk dance improved the participants' mental health.

Dancing is there for those who wish to engage in it, in whatever way they want, wherever they happen to be, and whether or not there is music is immaterial. You can make your own music because we know that **humming**, of itself, has therapeutic abilities.

Chapter 29: Walking Silently Is More Than You Think, So Don't Think

A ccording to a systematic review and meta-analysis, outdoor nature-based therapy (NBI) benefits all populations, including *healthy adults, older adults with long-term diseases,* and persons with common mental health issues. Nature-based treatments are effective for both *existing and preventing mental health issues.* When looking at mental health outcomes, the researchers found that *nature-based therapy given in groups had the **biggest and most consistent effects.***

From examining well-respected databases, they found 50 studies derived from 14,321 records. Those studies indicated that NBIs helped with a variety of mood issues, *including depression, anxiety, low self-esteem, and a lack of positive affect.* For most people with any mental health challenges, that about covers the field, right?

But two things need to be included here, and that is whether the individuals engaged in NBI *alone or in groups* and how that may have affected the outcomes. And, while engaged in NBI, were any of the *subjects told to free their minds from all thought* and allow themselves to "just be?"

The notion of "**just being**" closely aligns with Eastern philosophies and wellness practices, like *yoga, tai chi, qi gong,* and other exercise regimes, which primarily include *mindful breathing.* If you've wanted to try any of these, the Internet is a great place to explore what might be most helpful for you. I firmly believe in the power of visuals, and YouTube is my go-to for video tutorials on various topics. No, I don't get paid to make that statement; I believe it and use it myself.

A major public health burden is borne by mood-related disorders, including depression. Pharmacotherapy and psychotherapy (including cognitive behavioral therapy and psychoanalysis) are two examples of the more conventional approaches to treating mental health issues. But a study found that r*egular exercise and meditation improved participants' moods and reduced the severity of their symptoms when dealing* with mental health issues.

There is a mountain of evidence supporting the benefits of exercise for our neurobiology and general health. Even our brain health is improved by exercise and silence—two things we need to consider in our wish to be well and enjoy our lives.

There is a great deal of information showing how exercise and meditation can improve mood and may help reduce the risk of or symptoms of mental health issues. The specific guidelines for practicing exercise and meditation are still uncertain. Regardless of the variations in research methods, the results imply that everyone can profit from this.

How Silence Benefits Us

The development of new brain cells depends on an abundance of immature brain cells, which develop **more rapidly in quiet settings**. Following several days of relative quiet, these cells eventually can develop into **new neurons**. Doesn't that sound amazing that being quiet, contemplative and allowing your mind to wander a bit can cause the growth of new nerve connections or even cells? It is truly amazing.

White noise and Mozart's piano music, for example, both appear to have a beneficial effect at first, but they do not cause the same long-term increase in neuronal density as **silence**. Therefore, when it comes to preserving the brain and increasing its potential for neurological development, **silence is truly golden**.

Considering the importance of cognition upkeep in our modern minds, maybe we should rethink the value of silence when it comes to self-care. Too often, being silent, is misinterpreted as having some distress in our lives. We need to turn that around and see it as a time for reflection, refreshing or even engaging in some useful creativity. Unfortunately, we have an old saying that, *"An idle mind is the devil's workshop."* I totally disagree with that because I think an idle mind is a mind at work, and we should permit ourselves that "luxury" when we can—and we should find time for it.

How do you begin? The professionals advise starting with the basics:

1. Find a peaceful spot outside or in nature and go for a walk. Additionally, try to schedule it at a time when other people or activities won't interrupt you too much.

2. Before you do anything else, ensure you are not thirsty and hungry so you won't be distracted.

3. Remain alone with your thoughts, absent of all social activities: no phone, no walking companion, and no canine.

4. Pay attention to your emotions, breathing, and the breath-taking scenery. Focus on your breathing and the natural world, appreciating the sun's warmth.

Even without a forest or nature preserve, you can *find a peaceful spot* to go for a stroll. If you want to maintain mental silence in a city, it is up to you, not the surroundings. Get out into nature as much as possible, sit quietly for twenty minutes, and pay close attention to what you see.

Silent walking or even sitting in silence for a few minutes a day is the way to go and you can temper your time, your method and where you do it to suit your situation. Just remember that this is a simple, self-directed way to improve your mood and your mind at the same time. Don't be a prisoner to distraction and experience the pleasure of *doing nothing and not thinking for blocks of time.* It may take a little time, but you can do it.

Do you need to do this in one fell swoop? No, you can space it out over the day and stop and use it when you feel you might need a lift. It's like your coffee break for health, but there's no coffee involved here.

The time out you experience is well worth *any initial discomfort from thinking that you should always be actively doing something.* You are doing something: taking **care of yourself**.

Chapter Thirty

Chapter 30: Amazing Benefits of Crying

C rying is both a human and a universal trait. We may learn a lot about how people feel, manage, and express their emotions through crying since it is visceral, almost impossible to fake, and unlike any other kind of emotional expression. You can cry from the moment you are born until you are an adult.

There is a wide range of proneness to crying among adults, and people cry for different reasons and at various frequencies. As an **attachment activity,** crying is a critical component. Crying may help **alleviate stress** and, via psychobiological mechanisms, speed up the physiological and psychological **recovery processes following trauma**. Also, **others may feel compelled to help** the one crying if they see that they are in need, which could indirectly impact their own well-being.

As early as the Classical period, people began to recognize the therapeutic benefits of crying. Ancient Greeks and Romans believed our tears drain and cleanse us, much like a purgative. Modern psychological theory agrees, highlighting sobbing to *release pent-up emotions and stress.*

Because suppressing negative emotions (also known as "repressive coping") can have negative effects on mental and physical health, crying serves as a healthy outlet for these tough experiences. A weakened immune system, heart disease, high blood pressure, and mental health issues like worry, despair, and stress have all been associated with suppressive coping strategies, according to research. Research also shows that *crying enhances attachment behavior, fostering more empathy, support, and intimacy with loved ones.* Tears are the salve we crave when we have emotional wounds that need healing.

A Coping Mechanism

The psychological stress theory suggests that self-soothing, including crying, can be viewed as an emotion-focused coping strategy. This strategy, like response-focused emotion regulation, involves actions and thoughts aimed at addressing negative emotions head-on. People may resort to a range of adaptive and maladaptive activities to alleviate intense unpleasant or even pleasant emotions.

How our culture perceives crying is just as important as our own feelings and desires when deciding whether or not to cry. Crying less often in line with a country's level of individualism and collectivism might be enforced. So, crying, although helpful, could be viewed negatively.

Researchers anticipated a negative correlation between shame, masculinity/femininity, and mood swings. 16,800 male and 23,223 female students were surveyed across 30 nations. Their study revealed that masculinity/femininity, national wealth, shame, and crying frequency were significant predictors of mood change, all in the expected direction.

The findings point to the fact that **cultural norms** regarding crying and overall emotions of shame regarding crying impact how one feels following an incident of sobbing. But also remember that **correlation does not mean causation**, only that a statistical relationship appeared, and this may be spurious. Cultural norms change, however, and these changes often come by virtue of individuals pushing the limits of cultural acceptance.

Many people feel pressured to control their emotional reactions because of **expectations placed on them** by their social environments. This seems difficult on the surface, and research confirms that *acting against one's natural tendency is stressful.* Not crying when that would be our initial reaction to a situation, therefore, could be seen as harmful, both psychologically and physically, to us. Are we willing to pay that price, or should we be encouraged to cry when we need that emotional outlet?

Research suggests that crying may help preserve biological equilibrium, whether through unconscious modulation of heart rate or intentional self-soothing via deliberate breathing. We know that big boys do cry, and it's normal and healthy for them to do so.

Recent TV ads for programs aimed at helping sick or hungry children worldwide have now incorporated crying adults, both male and female, into their content. When ads utilize these societal changes, it would appear that the **times are changing** (thanks Bob Dylan).

Chapter 31: "Lighthouse Parents" and Raising More Confident Kids

Parenting styles have undergone many stylistic changes according to popular beliefs or individual cultural demands. Whether any of these styles is more appropriate for children's happy, healthy, and reassured development remains an open question.

Who dreams up these things? Call it clickbait or creativity. Whatever you choose, I tend to be cynical, and I think it is in the service of selling books or creating careers. I do not believe anyone should make a career out of addressing children's growth needs until **strong empirical evidence** supports that orientation. This raises concerns about Dr. Benjamin Spock's parenting books, **many of which his wife wrote** with scant research and no authorship acknowledgment.

Colleagues harshly criticized Spock's beliefs for mainly **depending on anecdotal evidence** rather than rigorous academic investigation. Were kids damaged when their mothers followed Dr. Spock's book for advice? We'll never know, but we believe his wife had good intentions and leave it at that.

We've had bulldozers, tigers, helicopters, jellyfish, scrunchies, Apple Watches, momfluencers, and gentle parents, to name only a few. It would seem that styles of parenting fluctuate as much as fashion. With so many opinions on good parenting, how can anyone know which approach is best for their child's future?

I used to work for a children's fashion magazine that promoted "Mothercraft," a notion **prevalent in the 1930s** but still being practiced in some places in the world, and certificates being awarded for completing courses. I never discovered the exact definition of Mothercraft, and the publication ceased mentioning it after the mid-20th century. It sounds like they were trying to make it more scientific, as so many people in the social sciences tried to make their professions more like the hard sciences.

Psychology students will recall how John Atkinson attempted to create a **formula for achievement**, and, of course, Freud tried to make his theory much like hard science, as did Carl Jung, too. Abraham Maslow, who failed in his attempts at two professions (law and medicine), finally devised a step theory of a *hierarchy of needs*.

Maslow's hierarchy of needs is an idea in psychology proposed by American psychologist Abraham Maslow in his 1943 paper. But there are unresolved issues here, too. Unanswered or questioned is how one can progress from step to step if one step is made impossible by economics or politics. In other words, each step along the way presents, sometimes inordinate challenges that cannot easily be met by anyone wishing to achieve self actualization. Maslow never addressed this, and it remains a problem that has not been fully responded to by people who are willing to accept his theory as is.

If the legends in psychological theory were trying to find a way forward in their profession, is it any wonder that parents are left wondering what to do? Parents were looking to the "authorities," who weren't such mavens in terms of raising healthy kids. Please don't accept as "authorities" anyone who has written a best-selling book. All it means is that they have effective marketing techniques, public relations, or agents who know how to work the system. Some have suggested that purchasing 10K copies of a book and giving them away will automatically make you a bestseller on some lists. It's the number, not the quality that counts.

Western parenting styles and the dynamics between parents and children have evolved significantly over the last several decades. These days, parents are less likely to yell at their kids and more likely to spend quality time with them and concentrate on communication and reasoning. For most parents, we have left behind the idea of spare the *"rod and spoil the child."* Corporal punishment is not an effective means of raising a healthy child.

However, there is **a lack of data** regarding the evolution of parental ideology throughout this time. I'm beginning to sound like Data in Star Trek, and for that, I must tip my hat to Dr. Lewis Terman, an eminent psychologist with a great sense of humor. Unfortunately, he was also an advocate of eugenics and racial inferiority. His doctoral dissertation dealt with seven "bright" or "stupid" students; we may have to give him a slight pass. Since the book is no longer under copyright, you can freely download and use it as you wish. However, it should be regarded as history rather than hard science per se.

Perfecting Parenthood

Everyone who is or will become a parent must realize that raising children requires thoughtful, practical solutions that can be applied to everyday obstacles. You will make mistakes and be sorry for them, but you will also help your children understand that **mistakes are a part of life.**

Parenting beliefs are understudied despite their influence on parenting activities. One significant belief and a particular aspect of self-efficacy is parental self-efficacy (PSE). Parental self-efficacy (PSE) is the conviction that a parent can benefit their child's growth and development.

Higher PSE scores correlate with less negative parenting and emphasizing children**'s strengths.** As with other parts of parenting, parents' views about their influence are not static but subject to change in response to internal and external influences. Different PSEs may emerge at the group level due to cultural and societal historical shifts.

Of course, cultural changes or shifts are also sensitive to the economic influences surrounding the parental group. It may not be a belief system but an *anxiety-reduction system* that permits more effective and humanistic behaviors toward children.

The proliferation of online communities and communication tools has unquestionably altered the role of parents and parenting styles. Between 1999 and 2014, the Internet became essential to Western society. It connects parents and exposes them to diverse parenting perspectives and may lead to the evolution of yet more styles of parenting.

A Google search for "parenting" in 2022, for instance, returned an abundance of results. One of the most common reasons parents use the internet is to **research topics related to parenting**. The vast majority of parents use the internet daily for this purpose. Research shows that moms' interest in *finding parenting resources* begins early in the pregnancy and continues to rise during the last trimester and in the weeks following delivery.

The Internet offers assistance and knowledge on various parenting concerns, which many parents appreciate. Many new mothers don't have experienced grandmothers around to offer reality-based, real-life experience and help in childcare and parenting. The good news? On-line resources can assist parents during the transition to parenting and shape their identities.

The Search for Answers

Now, the newest potential parenting style is lighthouse parenting. What are its central themes?

Explanations for lighthouse parenting are rather broad, with the basic underpinning being that parents *provide a stable force for the children* throughout their lives, which begins to grow through adolescence. In an age of too much information, we can easily find ourselves in a quandary as experts pull us to and fro, and we are left wondering what to do.

Some experts believe that parents' incessant online searching indicates that they are *feeling overwhelmed, burned out, and insecure* in their roles. That may be the case, and we, as parents, **are also looking for our lighthouses**. Should we, as adults or parents, forsake the guidance and help of others? Being an adult doesn't mean you need to give up everything and push it all aside to become the ultimate authority. That would be a mistake.

The emphasis here is to *permit the child **sufficient freedom to experience*** growth, development, and the wonder of life independently without **being overly protective**. Is this a new fad in parenting? Parenting responsibility and actions can't be fleeting, but they must have a solid foundation and individual beliefs associated with that style of parenting. As a child, I never realized the degree of independence my parents gave to me. It has proven to be a gift I will always treasure.

Children need most to **develop a sense of self-worth** and a belief that **challenges can be met** with reasonable resolution. All is not lost when something seems to be a failure, and it is here that parents need to contribute most with their reassurance. **Independence and problem-solving are** two things parents must strive to help their children develop.

We've also lived in a time when each child, engaged in all types of activities, was given an award for their participation. This idea has been discussed, and some believe it's a good idea, and some have contrary ideas about it. Does everything we do require a reward, and, if it does, can the rewards be internal rather than external and identified as some object given to us? We know that internal motivation *is far superior to momentary awards* that quickly lose their luster.

Recall Maslow and how he dealt with human development in terms of challenges in pursuit of self-actualization. If anyone provided an example of this, it was Maslow himself, who refused to give up and insisted upon working toward making himself better each day. He could have remained in his family's barrel-making business in New Jersey, but he pushed himself to greater heights, even in the face of what most saw as disappointments or failures. And *his relationship with his mother* was so contentious that he fled his Bar Mitzvah ceremony *rather than honor her.* We have to wonder what style of parenting she practiced.

Another example of someone who refused to give up in the face of physical disability was Dr. Milton **Erickson**, who, although partially paralyzed, perfected a form of hypnosis based on metaphors. Erickson's methods would lay the *groundwork for family therapy.*

Dr. Alfred Adler's work focused on the impact of childhood experiences and feelings of inferiority. Adler fought his sense of inferiority (he had rickets and several accidents as a child) as he helped others in what he believed was **our reason for being**. Rumors also circulated that Adler had **one arm shorter than the other,** which may have contributed to an early sense of inferiority.

Motivation issues are prevalent in psychological disorders, and they drive behaviors that make life more enjoyable or not, depending on the issue. Parents can significantly impact children's internal motivation and overall well-being, regardless of the current style of parenting being espoused, and this is where they can accomplish the most good.

The style used to achieve that end must not be faddish, and parents need to help themselves **to stop looking for the "answer"** to everything in their child's life. *There is no one answer for most things, and there is no one expert*. Everything must be dependent on the individual situation; therein lies the challenge.

Chapter 32: Smell Is One of the First Senses to Go in Alzheimer's, It's Not Always Cognition

With an estimated 32 million cases worldwide, Alzheimer's disease (AD) is one of the most common forms of dementia. It is *crucial to identify early indicators to screen populations at risk* and execute interventions promptly. There is a critical need for sensitive and early biomarkers to screen people for AD right now. One of the most encouraging sensory biomarkers **for AD** right now is **smell**.

When there is a loss of smell perception, identification, or memory, it is known as **olfactory dysfunction**. Often, we forget that one of our senses not only guides us to the enjoyment of life, but also can signal danger. Smell serves those purposes.

Our olfactory (smell) sense provides important information to the brain, but it is often overlooked compared *to visual and auditory abilities*. Researchers, however, have uncovered another fascinating aspect of our sense of smell. A *gradual decrease in smell sensitivity* is an early warning **sign of cognitive decline** and **structural brain alterations** associated with dementia and **Alzheimer's**.

Analysis of 515 seniors indicated that a *smell-test screening could detect cognitive impairment early*. As a national monitor for an Alzheimer's medication protocol, I saw smell sense testing provided to hundreds of patients across the US in a study several decades ago. So, it seems there was a belief that smell played a significant role in the early detection of this neurological disorder.

The rapid loss of smell is now being viewed as a potentially overlooked powerful predictor of what will happen anatomically in specific *brain areas*, and this work gives another clue. Before spreading to other brain regions, the characteristic *plaques and tangles of Alzheimer's disease* typically **manifest in areas related to smell and memory.**

But our sense of smell is one that can be negatively affected, and an area that needs to be considered is household cleaners. Recall a woman in an Alzheimer's clinical trial who had almost no sense of smell. Yes, she had a diagnosis of Alzheimer's, but when we delved deeper, we found that she had a constant need to clean her home with cleaning products that, when combined together, lodged an incredible assault on her ability to smell anything. The nose is a wonderful vehicle that leads directly to the brain, and it is here that the damage can occur.

Screening and smell sensitivity, as in the seniors mentioned previously, maybe helpful in warding off some forms of sense decrements, especially in smell. Odor discrimination and bilateral **hippocampal cortical thickness** (the major location for memory incorporation and maintenance) both improved after four months of training in repeated short-term sniffing of different odors. Researchers validated the results by conducting cognitive tests and magnetic resonance imaging (MRI) at baseline and follow-up periods. According to researchers, olfactory training has the potential to **prevent hippocampus atrophy** as an early intervention. But it's not limited to memory because the intervention has other benefits.

Several recent studies have shown that regular olfactory exposure, or "olfactory training" (OT), can improve mood by enhancing olfactory perception and *reducing the intensity of depressed symptoms*. Who knew that smelling a rose, brewing coffee, or other scents aids mental health and cognition? Anyone who believes in self-help techniques will surely want to read more on this fascinating approach to neurologic disorders.

Training Your Sense of Smell

A specialist in otolaryngology is the ideal person to consult for any comprehensive evaluation of your sense of smell. But if you are interested, you may test your nose's performance using a *few simple methods at home.* You can use everyday home items for self-evaluation or purchase a kit that uses sniff scratch cards.

You should still **see a physician for a proper evaluation**, but a home test can help you catch dips in your sense of smell.

Using what you already have around the house and the instructions from the SmellAbility Toolbox, you can **train your sense of smell** without spending a dime on oils. Essential oils are available in a vast array of perfumes, so you can use them if you prefer a particular set of fragrances. There's no lack of. aromatherapy stores and internet retailers selling them. Airtight containers can store essential oils for an extended period, making them a recommended and reliable source of fragrance.

Research on affordable, easy-to-implement, and efficacious home remedies for cognitive decline in the elderly is needed because it is becoming an increasingly serious problem in our society. One small research study examined whether healthy older persons might benefit from **nighttime olfactory enrichment** regarding cognitive function. People in the experiment group were given *seven distinct scents every week, one at night for two hours*, through an odorant diffuser. The experience with *minimum levels of odorant* was identical for individuals in the control group. Please refer to the original article (https://pubmed.ncbi.nlm.nih.gov/37554295/) for more detailed information on this specific research protocol.

The participants underwent functional magnetic resonance imaging (fMRI) scans and neuropsychological evaluations at baseline and six months into the trial. The **enriched group outperformed the control group** by a substantial margin of **226%**. The research suggests that administration of mild olfactory enrichment improves neural and cognitive performance. Therefore, olfactory enrichment **could be a low-effort strategy to improve brain health.**

However, it's important to remember that the weather or other pollutants in our homes *can affect our sense of smell*. If your sense of smell isn't as acute as you believe it should be, these factors may be entering into false positives. While not a researcher, you are interested in maintaining your cognition and mental health, which are connected to your sense of smell. Let your nose be your guide, but remember that an ENT physician visit may be needed for additional information and remedies.

Chapter
Thirty-Three

Chapter 33: Fire Up the Power of Art Therapies Against Stress and Help Yourself

A rtists have been prescribing remedies for people experiencing the symptoms of a mental illness since ancient Greece. Professionals with the proper credentials now employ the practice to aid those with a variety of mental health issues, including post-traumatic stress disorder (PTSD), anxiety, depression, and more.

Art therapy is a versatile approach that **does not necessitate high levels of artistic ability**. Each patient's demands will determine the art medium used in therapy, so it can be painting, drawing, sculpting or even needlework. Intentionally exposing you to non-traditional art materials (such as *tree branches and leaves*) may let you express yourself more fully. *Doodling, abstract designs, and contour drawing* are all ways to experiment with new ways of expressing yourself.

If you think doodling isn't helpful, consider the famous doodlers: Samuel Beckett; the poet and physician, **John Keats**, who doodled in the margins of his medical notes; **Sylvia Plath**; and the Nobel laureate (in literature, 1913) poet **Rabindranath Tagore**. Doodling was typical among US Presidents, including *Thomas Jefferson, John Quincy Adams, and John F. Kennedy*.

One of the most famous doodlers of all time was **Leonardo da Vinci**, who made copious notes and doodles in the margins of his notebooks. Just like the rest of us, Leonardo doodled *and scribbled; you* can see it in his digitized notebooks. But this prototypical Renaissance man, both unsurprisingly and characteristically, took that scribbling and doodling to a higher level entirely. His margin notes and sketches are not only elegant but also reveal his early insights into important subjects.

Doodling can help you process and visualize things. It may, unintentionally, spark some creativity that you didn't realize you possessed. Don't feel the need to be another Leonardo; this activity is about reducing stress, not adding to it by feeling competitive.

Depending on your requirements, art therapists **can guide you** in a form of creative expression. But even if you aren't working with an art therapist, using art yourself can prove a stress reducer.

In research studies utilizing art therapy, there was *less burnout and reduced work dissatisfaction* among the study's participants. Those who took part in the creative arts therapy program saw **reductions of 28% in anxiety, 36% in depression, 26% in PTSD, and 12%**

in emotional tiredness as a result of burnout. These enhancements persisted for a full year following the program's end. The use of art therapy has also been seen to help *healthcare professionals deal with their experiences of burnout.*

But while we know that art therapy works, how does it work in the brain? Researchers are posing this question and hope to answer it. One answer seems to be that it has the power to stimulate the activation of various *brain areas that may be involved in perception and emotion.*

And modern imaging techniques have improved our understanding of the many brain regions and functions involved in processing information. *Stimulating the senses is the most fundamental level of intervention* using **art mediums**.

The visual information processing system's ventral and dorsal branches handle visual feature recognition and spatial placement. Mood-state drawings capture the variations in brain region activation accompanying distinct emotional states. Art therapy provides an opportunity to work with fundamental sensory components for processing information and emotions. Even the most basic kinds of expression could provide a window into the brain's anatomy. It is an exciting opportunity for mental health and all forms of mental functioning.

But other than imaging, one other means of measuring stress is via the stress hormone cortisol levels in saliva. The biological basis of creative self-expression has been the subject of ongoing investigations. Salivary cortisol has been studied as a noninvasive biomarker and a surrogate for human stress experience.

No matter the participant's demographics, level of art experience, or preferred medium, the results show that **even a short art-making experience can have** a physiological effect on cortisol levels. The importance of this cannot be overstated, since we know that cortisol can be destructive at relatively consistently high levels. Research has shown that it can be involved in tissue damage.

Expressive writing has been associated with health benefits and reduced stress levels over the long run. There is some evidence that creative expression, such as through **music or painting**, can have a beneficial influence on physiological and mental health, similar to the effects of expressive writing.

An interesting aspect of writing is when you **use cursive form** rather than a computer or a typewriter. We know that many famous writers have produced their first drafts by hand on legal tablets. However, not many of them realized that the *very fact of moving their hand to produce letters and words has an important effect on their brain's* activities in areas where creativity may be sparked.

Cursive writing should ***never be dismissed*** as an **antiquated form of writing** and should be *included in your life and the education of children*, as I have noted in previous articles I have written on Medium. So, get a lined or unlined journal for yourself and begin this excellent doodling adventure or cursive writing exercises. Either one will benefit you.

Research has made the case for using art therapy, in any form, to assuage stress levels and improve mental and physical health. No matter the means used, individuals can benefit from anything from *writing to music to any form of art, such as* **painting, sculpting, or working with other mediums**.

I recall seeing a small film that was made for mental health professionals on how writing was a release for psychiatric patients. An older woman, in poor circumstances, began to write poetry on brown paper bags that she received at the supermarket when she went shopping. She couldn't afford to buy a journal or writing paper, but she found a way to write, and it provided incredible relief for her.

It is now **up to each of us to decide** which form is most appropriate for us as a stress-reduction method, and although professionals are available in the area of art therapy, that is not a mandate for us. *We can begin our form of therapy at any time we wish.*

Chapter 34: The Secret Body Material That No One Researched Much Until Now

M edical research swiftly pursued the secrets of our bodies, overlooking many facets of our physiology in this race; researchers are now surprised by the attention and potential of one unstudied aspect. What exactly is this mysterious substance, and why **do you need to know about it**? New research is beginning to study this hidden neural network deep in this tissue, and it would seem to have promise.

The mysterious material is called **fascia**, and fascia isn't just an **empty sack** of tissue that *holds muscles and nerves together* but is much more complex. Fascia contributes to our *body's stability and enables us to stand upright, move smoothly,* and maintain other areas *yet to be discovered.*

Fascia is practically inseparable from all structures in the body because it enhances function and support by creating continuity among tissues. Researchers have recently resolved the nomenclature difficulties caused by the historically challenging study of fascia. The goal of one research group was to review current literature on fascia, consolidate studies on fascia advancements, and *address concerns with fascia terminology, descriptions, and clinical significance.*

How could researchers have missed all of their findings for so many years? Perhaps we need to consider that this specific type of biological tissue was thought to be insignificant in studying other parts of our bodies. Now, a practical system for classifying fascia divides them into **four types:** *connecting, fascicular, compression, and separating fasciae.* Each of these types has specific functions:

1. **Connecting fascia:** *Links muscles, organs, and other structures.* It provides a framework for bodily organization and assists in force transmission between body parts.

2. **Fascicular**: This membrane surrounds and separates muscle fibers and bundles. It allows individual *muscle fibers to slide against each other* and supports blood vessels and nerves within muscles.

3. **Compression fascia**: It *creates compartments* to contain and support muscles and organs, helps *maintain the shape and position of body structures, and* generates and transmits tension.

4. **Separating fascia**: Divides *different muscle groups or organs*, reduces friction between adjacent structures, and *facilitates independent movement of body parts*

Based on preliminary research, indications now point toward *aspects of our emotions and cognition* that are involved in our development and current existence in unknown ways. Of course, *neglecting to maintain the delicate structure of the fascia also* leads to a downside.

But how do we know that we must play a role in maintaining this tissue if we and professionals never gave it much consideration? **No one has enlightened us about the importance of fascia.**

What input can we engage in to retain the structure? Research points to how important it is to *recognize this structure and constantly work on its health* to help us maintain our physical and mental health. We realize the importance of this maintenance when we **consider pain in our joints or the inability to straighten up** after we have worked at our computer. Fascia tissue *plays a role in both* and in many other aspects of our lives, and we can no longer ignore it or not take responsibility for **our input.**

Fascia and Mental Health

Research has now shown that fascia tissue, in some areas, is rich in neurologic connections and may be amenable to change through imagery. It is also suggested that *mental states of emotion and cognition* may also be related to this tissue. Who would have thought that an insignificant tissue pushed aside in research would have proven to be so important?

One area of new consideration deals with how we might be able to have some power over these tissues. The suggestion now is to use the term "fascial mental imagery" (FMI) to describe a subtype of MI (mental imagery) that centers on the various aspects of fascial tissue, including its position, structure, physiology, and mobility. Dynamic neuro-cognitive imagery (DNI), sometimes called "The Franklin Method," is one way being considered to use FMI. Remember, this is something that is being considered, it is not necessarily heavily researched as a method.

The biopsychosocial model, based on psychology theories, explains the facial relationships in detail as a result of the complicated interaction of biological, psychological, and social elements. Changes to the myofascial continuum *may be associated with increased pain sensitivity.* It is believed that the myofascial continuum also plays a role in both **depressive disorders and chronic pain**.

Unfortunately, there is a *notable lack of understanding of the association* between chronic pain, depression, and particular fascial characteristics, even if the myofascial continuum is being more acknowledged as a possible contributor to these disorders. Researchers compared people with and without **chronic neck pain and depression**, finding significant differences in their fascial characteristics. The results of the study appear to provide compelling evidence that facial *features might be crucial in the setting of depressive disorders and persistent pain.*

Exercise plays an important role in cognitive decline. Multiple studies of this role involved 341,471 subjects. Cognitive impairment or deterioration was *less common among those who regularly engaged in physical activity.* By the way, which tissues get activated during physical activity? **The fascias, of course**.

A Few Ideas for Maintenance

Research in the field points to several specific ways we might engage in certain activities that would benefit our various types of fascia tissue and improve our health. Remember, however, that *there is insufficient, robust research at this point*, and suggestions are simply that—suggestions, not steps to be taken as a regular ritual. Before engaging in any exercise or program that involves these activities, make sure to seek approval from your primary physician or rehabilitation therapist.

1. **Perform regular fascial release:** Consider using a foam roller or massage ball on tight areas Apply pressure to restricted tissues

2. **Incorporate plyometric exercises**: Include skipping, hopping, and burpees in your routine. The aim is to boost the body's elastic recoil capacity

3. **Practice agility training**: Add lateral shuffling, zigzag running, and quick forward/backward movements, and consider activities like jumping rope or playing hopscotch

4. **Engage in slow, dynamic stretching**: Perform exercises like walking lunges, squats, and arm circles

5. **Reduce prolonged inactivity**: Avoid sitting for extended periods *Take regular breaks from desk work* or smartphone use

6. **Vary your movements**: Avoid repetitive motions. Incorporate a diverse range of activities in yourroutine

7. **Stay consistent**: Maintain these practices regularly for optimal fascial health

One of the hidden mysteries of the human body has now been revealed in some of its highly intricate activities, and we have new information that will enable us to *maintain our health in simple ways*. Who knows what else we may find out about the specific types of fascia and how healthcare professionals might utilize them further to improve our quality of health into our later years?

Chapter Thirty-Five

Chapter 35: Love's Not So Simple But Complex

C ouples dating wait for that special moment when one will whisper that highly desirable and long-waited-for statement, "**I love you**." Their understanding of love may differ from the love we all will experience. Researchers are now *digging deep into the entire issue of love and* finding more than we ever knew.

How many types of love do you think there are? Most of us might say t*he love of children, parents, friends, lovers, and even our country,* but would that encompass all the love researchers are finding? We need to understand the concept of love and how it affects us physically and, as a result, emotionally.

Different love affects different areas of the brain and different neurotransmitters—those pesky little chemical messengers that make it all possible. If we can boil it all down to neurotransmitters, are we then predicting that there might be something as simple as the words in that song, "Love Potion Number Nine?" Do we need to find Madame Rue and her herbal concoctions? Or do we need to use more sophisticated means of stimulating love? As some researchers believe, are there six, seven, or ten different loves? Here's where the complexity enters the stage.

Certain research also suggests the common belief that "**love is blind**" is true. According to research, the brain's attachment and reward networks are activated when we experience maternal and romantic love. Similar to how these ancient brain areas are involved in parental caregiving and long-term bonding in other mammals, they are also involved in these processes in our species. When we love something, is it neurologically the same as loving nature or our child?

Six Types of Love

Researchers, using story simulations and MRI technology, have concluded that love objects *stimulate multiple areas of the brain. This discovery reveals* six different types of love **based on the target of affection**.

Feelings of love for six different objects asserted are:

1. romantic partners,

2. one's children,

3. friends,

4. strangers (varieties of interpersonal love),

5. pets (interspecies love), and 6. nature (nonsocial love).

How does the brain decide which to stimulate to provide the appropriate type of love specific to that object? Three partially overlapping brain networks make up the "global human connection system": the reward-motivation system, the embodied simulation/empathy network, and the mentalizing system. This system categorizes closer affiliative relationships (parent-child, romantic, and friend) according to three factors: *salience, social cognition, and social reward.*

There are subtle differences between close interpersonal relation-ships—especially romantic and parent-child love—and more remote kinds of love for strangers, pets, and the natural world, according to stories and recordings provided byMRI. Interpersonal love of all types stimulated brain parts *linked to social cognition*, or "theory of mind." The domains of reward and social cognition, as well as those connected to *compassion or altruism,* seemed to be implicated in the love of strangers. Owners of pets exhibited brain activity comparable to that of *interpersonal affection.*

Pets, too, play an important, integral role in these love relationships. Research to date has shown this to be true. *Strong social ties and love are well-known to act as buffers against adversity.* Humans and animals frequently **develop closer relationships**.

A dynamic and mutually beneficial relationship between people and animals is called the "human-animal link." Whether pets are beneficial to people's health and well-being has long been a source of debate in human-animal interaction(HAI). At present, inquiries focus on *who, what, and why questions for certain situations* and not for others.

What About Singles?

Many types of love exist, and, in fact, even those who are not ro-mantically attached at the moment, i.e., single, can be segregated into distinct groups, where some are happier than others. So being single does not mean you are either lonely or unloved.

The 4,835 adults who were unattached at the time of one study ranged in age from 18 to 65. The poll found **ten different subsets of singles**, with some subsets reporting higher levels of happiness than others.

One in five adults who were single *reported being overjoyed.* Their level of happiness was identical to that of the happiest couples in previous research. The survey revealed that 40% of the singles were satisfied, 36% were somewhat satisfied, and **10% were very unhappy**.

The majority of singles, contrary to common belief, reported high levels of happiness and life satisfaction. Therefore, contrary to popular belief, being single can be just as fulfilling as being in a committed relationship, dispelling the myths that surround being single.

Is love complicated? Undoubtedly, it is more involved than we may have previously considered it to be. Depending on the type of love involved, it engages unique and interconnected networks and sections of the brain. Some portions of our love are *based on reward areas*, while others are more involved in altruistic connections.

One area of love researched by many is that of pets and their place in our lives as not only objects of love but seemingly *aids in resilience and helping when adversity* comes into our lives.

Chapter 36: Parental Stress Has a Serious Impact on Children

Childhood is mythically a time of wonder, exploration, and parental love, but is that always the case? Recent research is pointing in another direction, and it involves parental stress and its effect on children. Although there are many benefits to being a parent, there are also many **demands and difficulties**, such as dealing with *teenagers, sleepless nights, temper tantrums, financial challenges, and relationship problems*. Parents of children younger than 18 regularly *report higher levels of stress* compared to the general population.

A study that examined data from the American Psychological Association's Stress in America survey over a decade found that in 2023, one-third of parents reported high levels of stress, compared to a much smaller percentage of the general population (20%). While parents are experiencing more significant stress, what effect might it have on their children?

Roughly three million German children lived with a parent who suffered from a mental disorder. Compared to children whose parents do not have mental illness, those whose parents have a history of mental illness are *three to seven times more likely to exhibit subclinical symptoms*, have a lower quality of life concerning health, and have inferior academic achievement.

Aside from classroom activities, where parents may be most involved at home with homework, reading, and assignments, parental involvement may be vital in another area: extracurricular sports activities. The highly stressed parent may not provide this involvement. Children who are involved in extracurricular activities outperform their non-participating classmates and face less of a disadvantage in the classroom. Parents' participation in athletic activities is associated with improved academic performance in their children. How can sports activities contribute to a child's development?

Sports act through the mediating role of higher well-being indicators, including mental toughness, *strength-based coping techniques, and perseverance*, which positively correspond to higher academic performance. Athletic participation is associated with cognitive abilities, self-confidence, competitive spirit, and a sense of duty.

While youth sports are encouraged for children, and parents also value involvement, is there *a point where sports exhibit a downside*? Do sports activities have a downside, despite encouraging them for children and the value parents place on involvement? Such psychological effects will not go without consequences in the future.

Competing in athletic events has split opinion among experts. Some argue that it is *too serious, too cutthroat, and too controlled by adults*, while others claim it is *great for teaching kids discipline and teamwork*. Peer-reviewed research has also voiced concerns regarding the physiological and psychological pressures commonly linked to youth sports.

The Stressed Parent and Individual Children's Activities

Aside from not being capable, psychologically and physically, of encouraging, participating in, and facilitating children's extracurricular activities, the highly stressed parent may promote disturbances in the children's psychological well-being. The situation has risen to such a height of concern that the US Surgeon General has provided a message, both of concern and of possible remediation for the stressed parent.

The Surgeon General indicated that, "For all parents and caregivers to thrive, the advisory urges a *change in culture, policy, and programs*. As a nation, more must be done to help parents and caregivers by changing social mores to *create an environment where these individuals are respected, valued, and given agency over their children and the challenges they face.* This advisory expands upon previous efforts to guarantee families receive necessary assistance, *such as advocating for more paid family leave, enhancing childcare and early childhood education, and providing unprecedented funding for mental health treatment."*

Legislative reforms, community activities, and individual actions can help parents and caregivers ease stress and improve their mental health and well-being. The Surgeon General's Advisory *pro-*

vides guidelines for stakeholders, including employers, neighborhoods, community groups, and schools.

The guidelines are essential. The future of any country depends not on individuals alone, but on family units, the manner in which parents are viewed, and in which children are raised. If we permit mental health issues to fester in parents in need, we are lighting a fire that will inflame children's abilities to progress and, instead, leave them in ashes.

The metaphor may be somewhat distressing, but so are the consequences of unintentional or unattended mental health issues regarding parental stress. We owe it to our children, and we owe it to the parents who are raising them. Doing less is not acceptable in a country that has much to offer.

Chapter
Thirty-Seven

Chapter 37:
Food Dyes Play
What Role in
Any Mental
Disorders?

Working in the food marketing industry many years ago, I learned how product placement *and packaging colorings* were essential to achieving product success over competitors. Certain colors were seen as more attractive than others, and **red was one color that stood out**.

Update: "Red 3 is used in nearly 3,000 food products, according to a database by one environmental health group, including

Pez, Peeps, Betty Crocker's products, and Dubble Bubble chewing gum. Like other food dyes, it adds nothing of nutritional value and is used instead to add color to foods for marketing purposes," from The Guardian newspaper.

Now we know that coloring on packages isn't the only place it plays a major role. Food coloring is like lush flowers to waiting honeybees, but in this instance, those waiting and *attracted to the colors are children*. How often have you seen a child with a parent and a grocery cart where the child insists they want a specific cereal or candy? It happens every day.

The ability of synthetic food colors to impact sensory appeal and promote a preference for specific meals is widely believed to have several effects on consumers, particularly children. Children are more prone to developing diseases such as *cancer, allergies, mutations, cytotoxicity,* and clastogenic activities, which are all linked *to these color additives*. Other symptoms include *changes in behavior in kids* with and without medical diagnoses, as well as problems with the *digestive and respiratory systems*.

But not only the colorings but also the manufacturing of certain foods can cause something that is, as of now, undiagnosed: a *specific food addiction*. Ultra-processed foods are formulated to keep you coming back, so food coloring and processing are key to consumer attraction.

Currently, **Red 40, Green 3, Blue 1, Blue 2, Yellow 5, and Yellow 6** are some of the dyes that have recently come under fire from concerned parents and teachers who point to the *few studies* that have shown a connection between these colors and negative behavioral issues in children, such as impulsivity, *depression, aggression, and ADHD*. Indeed, based on the evidence available to them, California legislators are currently considering banning certain dyes and ingredients in lunches served **to children in schools.**

Why Some and Not Others?

Due to the behavioral pattern known as Avoidant/Restrictive Food Intake Disorder (ARFID), individuals with Autism Spectrum Disorder are more susceptible to the harmful effects of food additives. Because these children's interests are typically stereotyped and they tend to maintain repetitive eating patterns, **often based on colors**, accepting some foods while rejecting others, this disorder manifests itself through a variety of eating behaviors, including *overeating, severe restrictions, and even the complete avoidance of certain foods.* Color plays a major role in the food selection and restriction of these individuals.

The California Office of Environmental Health Hazard Assessment (OEHHA) examined past and current research and applied advanced risk assessment methods to interpret the findings. Researchers included studies in the risk evaluation that monitored youngsters' behavior while on a dye-free diet for multiple weeks.

After giving the children food or liquids with added dyes, the researchers employed a variety of standardized procedures to record their behavior. The research results provided ample evidence for legislators to consider drafting proposals banning certain colorings in food served in school cafeterias.

According to the OEHHA results, synthetic food colors can cause *hyperactivity and other neurobehavioral disorders* in some children. Children's sensitivity to these dyes, however, varies.

Research has shown that synthetic *food dyes can impact certain youngsters* more than others. Research on animals has found that synthetic food dyes alter brain *structure and function at the microscopic level and impact learning, memory, and activity*. We must consider whether we can extrapolate these studies with animals to human behavior, which poses a serious question.

What About Red Dye?

A widely used color additive is Red Dye 40. Packaged foods typically include coloring agents in their ingredients list. Keep in mind that **food labels indicate ingredients by weight; therefore**, it is better to read labels before eating.

Among its many names, Red Dye 40 is Lake Red 40, FD&C, and Red 40 Aluminum Lake (FD&C Red №40) and Red №40.

Cakes, icing, pastries, cereals, gum, yogurt, puddings, gelatins, ice cream, popsicles, soda, energy drinks, sports drinks, protein powders, chips, and salty snack foods are among the items that **typically include Red 40**. If you want to avoid ingesting any food product that contains this dye, carefully read the ingredients list and note how much of the dye is by seeing *where it is listed in the order of ingredients*.

Research has also demonstrated that synthetic food colors can disrupt the brain's natural *serotonin and dopamine balance*. Depression and anxiety disorders are linked to imbalances in the neurotransmitter serotonin, which is involved in mood regulation. In a similar vein, dopamine is involved in pleasure and reward pathways, and changes in dopamine levels can exacerbate mood disorders.

Inflammation and oxidative stress, according to other research on artificial food colors, may *worsen anxieties and depression*. A number of mental health conditions mentioned here have been associated with chronic inflammation and oxidative stress.

In an age where artificial colorings have become endemic to our food chain, it may be challenging to exclude those that do contain these ingredients. Those wishing to exclude questionable ingredients have opted to change their diets to more organic products, fresh foods, and vegetables and take great care whenever purchasing packaged products.

It would appear to be a wise choice, *but it is an individual choice* based on personal experience. As one of my professors once told our class, research can *be done on a sample of only one, and* that can be valid. So, if you are noticing changes such as those included here that may be related to food coloring, you *can take whatever action you believe is necessary* for maintaining your mental and physical health.

Chapter 38: Worried About Cognitive Decline? Study Offers an Indicator That May Help

Where did you put your keys? Whose birthday is coming up? What's that movie star's name? All these questions we can easily and quickly answer, except when we can't, and then it's what my patient asked, "*Doc, do you think I'm getting 'old-timer's disease?*"

Well, I knew he meant Alzheimer's, and, no, I didn't think he was getting it, and *too many people are jumping to conclusions* when they have
one of these slips of memory. For that man, he was under inordinate
stress in his life, and all of the stressors combined were causing him to
have difficulty with his memory. That's not unusual because we know
that stress interferes with memory formation or recall.

Do you know *I sometimes can't remember a friend's name* when
needed? Or that I once sat on a TV set with Bill O'Reilly for his show,
and I wanted to ask him a question, but *I couldn't remember that his
name is "Bill"?*

Know how I felt? I didn't think it was Alzheimer's because I've had
this problem for *my entire life*. Despite having solid clues that I use, my
clues still fail me, just like when I try to recall the name of a publishing
company that published one of my books. I tell myself, "*What do
you do when you jump up?*" The answer, of course, is "spring," but it
doesn't always come so quickly.

But things like this, especially for anyone who's had it for their
entire lives, don't mean that I or anyone else has a form of dementia
known as aphasia. For whatever reason, my brain isn't embedding
people's names where they're supposed to be stored, and I have to
live with it. I have used all of the memory techniques that have been
suggested by numerous professionals, and *none of them work reliably
for me*.

The only one that worked, or works partially for me, is **the clue
one,** and, as you can see, that's not always something on which I
can depend. For example, I have a neighbor named Joe, and his wife
recommended that if I just think of "***cup of Joe***," *the term often used
for coffee*, I might be able to remember his name. Well, guess what? **It
works all the time for me**. Forever, he shall be "cup of Joe."

Of course, not remembering, for various reasons, is part of being human. However, remembering everything is not the unique gift we might think it is. Whenever you think that having an incredible memory is something you would treasure, think of the unfortunate case of Alexander Luria's study of Solomon Shereshevsky, also known simply as "S."

Luria wrote about this man's **inability to forget** in his famous book, The Mind of a Mnemonist. He could recall and recite word-for-word pages of text he had been shown decades earlier. *It is one of the most extraordinary examples of an inability to forget.* Some people do have an extraordinary ability to remember things, especially printed pages and we note they have eidetic memory, often also called photographic memory. The psychologist, Dr. Joyce's Brothers, did have that type of memory, which served her well when she went on to win a TV game, The $64,000 Question, where her topic was boxing.

One of the Long-Term Studies

Just as there is a famous, ongoing, and long-term study of heart disease and longevity (the intergenerational Framingham Heart Study), other studies are decades long. One study that comes to mind, one of my postgraduate professors took part in, is Donald Super's career choice study, which began in 1951 and studied boys in the eighth or ninth grade in elementary school into their adult years and their careers. Fortunately, it doesn't seem that super included any components of memory into his study, but there must have been some. In fact, one of my university professors noted that her father was in a specific profession, and that was one reason she began to study careers. So, she had a memory of her father's work, and then she wanted to delve more into it.

Much of the work done by popular writers in terms of stages of people's lives in terms of their careers or perspective about their future had initial research available to them from the Super study. Researchers have conducted many other studies in the area of genetics, cognition, and specific diseases, such as the Nurses Health Study of breast cancer, for multiple decades.

Of course, in the area of studies, a particular study of memory stands out: The Nun Study by Dr. David Snowdon. The study of nuns in a cloistered convent in the Midwestern United States detailed evaluations of their lifestyles, prior education, and current activities in a group who agreed to donate their brains for Alzheimer's research. Altogether, *678 nuns ages 75 to 107 took part* in the study. The study results were also available to consumers in Snowdon's book, Aging with Grace.

The Rush Memory and Aging Project (MAP) was started in 1997 in Illinois. It focuses on gathering information from 910 individuals who have maintained their abilities. The study mainly involved participants, and annual assessments monitored their neurological, cognitive, physical, and emotional well-being over a span of up to fourteen years.

While there is some evidence linking lower psychological well-being to an increased risk of dementia, how our psychological well-being changes as dementia progresses remains unknown. Six dimensions of psychological well-being were measured yearly: *self-acceptance, autonomy, environmental mastery, purpose in life, positive relations with others, and personal progress.*

One component of well-being is **having a sense of purpose in life.** An analysis indicated that a *decreased risk of dementia* was associated with a purpose in life. This aligns with previous findings from the Rush Memory and Aging Project (MAP), which showed that a **higher sense of meaning in life** was associated with a decreased likelihood of developing moderate cognitive impairment (MCI) or dementia and might increase the time without dementia.

In addition, a higher degree of psychological wellness may lessen the cognitive impairments caused by Alzheimer's disease, which has been associated with rapid cognitive decline. *The fact that people with dementia frequently struggle to adapt to new circumstances, set new goals, and maintain old connections may have an impact on psychological health.*

Purpose and Happiness

According to previous studies, there are *social, behavioral, and biological routes* by which well-being protects health. Similarly, there may be processes that connect well-being to a reduced risk of dementia. A good example is the correlation between *happiness and increased social engagement,* which helps with cognitive function and staves off dementia, according to the available studies.

An increase in happiness can improve mental and neurological health, which in turn encourages healthier lifestyle choices like quitting smoking and increasing physical exercise. Studies have also shown that those with *higher levels of well-being have better cardiovascular functioning,* which lowers their risk of dementia. Is happiness a factor in warding off dementia? The World Happiness Report appears to be veering in that direction. The website offers the complete report for download.

As they say, often in jest, "*Let a smile be your umbrella on a rainy day.*" Studies to date have shown that a sense of purpose brings happiness, which can be **one of your major assets** in maintaining your cognitive health. The recommendations, therefore, are simple: find **your purpose and stick to it**, and you will help yourself. *Purpose is the motto of a life well lived.* Supporting the well-being of individuals with dementia and their caregivers requires activities and settings that enhance well-being.

I know one woman who, to celebrate her 85th birthday, decided to explore activities that few of her age would consider. *She not only went on a very long zip line in Central America* but also *went skydiving* and had a photo taken of her in free fall.

She continues to find new purpose in life in the assisted living facility, where she has proven to be a leader for those who may have felt lost and warehoused. Her spirit and energy continue to encourage others to live life as fully as they can physically. She has also improved her well-being and found a new purpose that can only benefit her as she leads others in *performing plays, creative writing activities, and trips* into the surrounding area to explore the environment. To date, she is now 92 and still active.

We can be our best mental and physical health advocates if we follow the most straightforward rule: **find a meaningful purpose for ourselves**.

Chapter 39: The Beast of Fear Ruling Your Life Can Be Vanquished

A *nxieties are hardwired into our neurological systems*. Our fear reaction (a.k.a. anxiety) is a survival strategy that warns *us to stay vigilant* and stay away from hazardous circumstances or things. Anything from unsettling noises we hear when we are alone and in the dark to the growl of a dangerous animal approaching, feared places or objects, or authoritarian people in our lives *can set it off*. But we must remember that the basis for fear keeps us safe *once we realize where the fear comes from and use ways to manage it*.

However, we jeopardize our safety when we allow our fears to take over without real dangers. Those who have experienced extreme or potentially fatal stress may develop a heightened sensitivity to danger, even in seemingly harmless circumstances. This kind of *widespread anxiety is harmful to our mental health* and can lead to serious, long-term problems. And there are specific portions of our brains that respond to fear.

Researchers believe fear is **not limited to one sense or one area of our brains.** There is more than one facet to fear. Memory plays a role, too. For example, there is some evidence that the perception of aerial predators triggers fear actions through a circuit involving a single brain area. I knew a woman who had an excessive fear of birds, even small ones, and went outside if a bird came near her, she flew into a panic and tried to hide from it.

The brain's chemical messengers, or neurotransmitters, flip a switch in response to acute stress-related fear. A *generalized fear response occurs when the chemical signals switch* from creating excitatory to inhibitory neurotransmitters. The neurons that undergo this transition are connected to areas of the brain that are known to be involved in fear responses.

As an interesting side note, researchers showed that blocking the production of this chemical *could prevent generalized fear responses.* But isn't that what pharmacologic interventions do now? **Yes, that's exactly what they do,** but there are other ways besides medications to help ourselves.

Don't Depend on Chemistry

Evidence from meta-analyses of large-scale research shows that mindfulness-based therapies (MBIs) have a moderate impact on reducing symptoms of anxiety and dread. This effectiveness was comparable to that of cognitive behavioral therapy and other well-established treatments for anxiety. Many other health issues and ailments have found therapeutic applications for MBIs beyond anxiety disorders. These include *depression, social functioning, prosocial behavior, pain, sleep difficulties, and problems experienced by cancer patients.*

During these research programs, participants learn mindfulness techniques to help them *pay more deliberate attention, change how they interact with their thoughts, and practice nonjudgmental coping mechanisms* when faced with negative emotions or thoughts. Now that we know that it is possible to help ourselves, what should we begin to do?

In cases where patients may have **highly distressing illnesses**, such as cancer, specific interventions, such as tai chi/qigong, have proven effective in *both anxiety and depression as well as pain control.* These ancient and simple physical exercises seem to permit the mind and the body to act as one in combating fear, a.k.a. anxiety, and depression. Just as yoga can distract from anxiety and increase attentiveness to the present moment, patients can find these exercises, which have been used for thousands of years in Asia, useful. Some people begin a morning routine to start their day off, while others may use it later in the day.

<u>Work-related Anxiety</u>

We call it anxiety when we're at work. Still, *it's actually a fear response* because many things come into play, such as the *need to meet deadlines, the attitudes of supervisors and coworkers, the wish to succeed, feelings of incompetence, a.k.a. the imposter syndrome*, and others you may recognize in your workplace. Of course, these things are also commonly experienced at home, albeit under different circumstances, and not viewed as "work."

>   1. The first thing we want to do is **recognize the fear** and what is causing it. Expressing it in words can help make it

more manageable, and discussing it with a trusted friend can provide a new perspective.

2. Another way of handling fear is to **reframe it from something** highly charged with negative emotions **into an opportunity**. Remember, not everything is one-sided. *Look for the benefits*, and you may find something that *raises your mood and changes your outlook.*

3. Practice mindfulness or simple relaxation exercises throughout the day. *Don't limit your relaxation* to just one specific time; use it throughout the day *to manage any anxiety or fear before it takes hold.*

4. If you find yourself with a task that seems overwhelming, remember that every task **involves many small steps** to achieve its end. Analyze and use those steps to approach the resolution with everything in place, especially your emotional well-being.

5. Utilize a network of coworkers or friends who can help you think things over, suggest options, and provide different perspectives. Just as one textbook may not help you learn a subject, one person may be less helpful than a group acting on your behalf.

6. Whenever you feel fear, you have resources you can *use in advance* or at that moment. **You have power**, so use it and recharge it regularly. Be sure to begin doing the tai chi exercises. **Begin them now** and make them a regular part of your life, and you will benefit from them.

Many people do tai chi outside in the morning before the work of the day begins. What a wonderful way to begin the day with relaxation and exercise that can make the day more positive.

Chapter 40: The Many Faces of PTSD and You May Have It

The first reference I ever saw to a mental health disorder, PTSD, was right after the Vietnam War, when a young military psychiatrist wrote a thin paperback intended for professionals. I had never heard of this disorder, and, I suspect, neither did many others, but wasn't there a disorder during World War II, Shell Shock?

Words like "soldier's heart," "*shell shock*," and "*war neurosis*" originated in earlier battles. That second diagnosis was the same as the névrose de guerre and Kriegsneurose that were used in the scientific literature of Germany and France. Is weren't. new disorders, but ones that had usually been dismissed and seen as physical frailty or psychological weakness in a soldier. Therefore, they carried with them an excessive degree of shame for anyone who had the symptoms.

PTSD isn't a **recent phenomenon**; it has a history associated with it. Beginning in the American Civil War (1861–1865) and the Franco-Prussian War (1870–1871), there were official medical efforts to treat the issues faced by combat veterans. An additional contribution to our prior knowledge of trauma-related disorders came from European accounts of the mental effects of train accidents. Today, it is not unusual for people in *car, plane, or railroad accidents* or natural disasters, such as *floods, volcanic eruptions, or wildfires,* to have PTSD. I once worked in a healthcare practice where many individuals with PTSD after car accidents came for therapy.

The first person I had ever known who received a diagnosis of **shell shock** after he returned from World War II was a friend's relative. The man felt so overwhelmed with anxiety when they shipped him overseas to join the battle that he couldn't disembark from the landing craft and experienced absolute panic. He literally froze.

Instead of sending him to the front line, they sent him to a military hospital and then immediately shipped him home. He never left his house again for the remainder of his life after he got back. He received no treatment and no medication because he and his family saw it as a horrific shame on all of them. When he required a haircut, the barber came to the house. Anxiety disorders ran in the family, and several of them experienced shy bladder syndrome, also known as *paruresis*.

The following person I would meet, who had PTSD, was a woman who *narrowly escaped death during the attack on the Twin Towers on September 11, 2001,* in New York City, where she worked. Her fear was so great that she could not enter Manhattan from the nearby state where she lived, and she said it was impossible to even think about visiting the memorial built there. Typically, while walking in her neighborhood, something would trigger fear and panic, and she would *try to hide in a store doorway* or *against a wall.* She had **atypical fits of anger** and prejudice toward people of different ethnicities, *something she had never experienced before.* Even volunteering at a church food pantry became too much for her.

Imagine how this affected her; she never returned to work. Tragically, she contracted three different cancers from exposure at the site of the attack on that day, and she died because of them.

I also met a woman whose husband had repeatedly beaten her about the head. Now, she suffers from episodic seizure disorder, but she did not allow that to stop her from getting a college degree. However, it affected her memory, and she needed to be reassured because her self-esteem was fragile. Fortunately, she exited the marriage and is now flourishing with her son and her new career.

The usual symptoms of PTSD are well-known and documented in the literature, as well as in the DSM (Diagnostic and Statistical Manual of Mental Disorders). The National Institute of Mental Health delineates them as follows:

*"**To be diagnosed with PTSD, an adult must have all of the following for at least 1 month:***

- *At least one re-experiencing symptom*
- *At least one avoidance symptom*
- *At least two arousal and reactivity symptoms*
- *At least two cognitive and mood symptoms*

Re-experiencing symptoms

- *Flashbacks — reliving the traumatic event, includingphysical symptoms, such as a racing heart or sweating*
- *Recurring memories or dreams related to the event*
- *Distressing thoughts*
- *Physical signs of stress*

Thoughts and feelings can trigger these symptoms, as can words, objects, or situations that are reminders of the event.

Avoidance symptoms

·   *Staying away from places, events, or objects that are reminders of the experience*

·   *Avoiding thoughts or feelings related to the traumatic event*

Avoidance symptoms may cause people to change their routines. For example, some people may avoid driving or riding in a car after a serious car accident.

Arousaland reactivity symptoms

·   *Being easily startled*

·   *Feeling tense, on guard, or on edge*

·   *Having difficulty concentrating*

·   *Having difficulty falling asleep or staying asleep*

·   *Feeling irritable and having angry or aggressive outbursts*

·   *Engaging in risky, reckless, or destructive behavior*

Arousal symptoms are often constant. They can lead to feelings of stress and anger and may interfere with parts of daily life, such as sleeping, eating, or concentrating.

Cognitionand mood symptoms

·   *Trouble remembering key features of the traumatic event*

·   *Negative thoughts about oneself or the world*

·   *Exaggerated feelings of blame directed toward oneself orothers*

·   *Ongoing negative emotions, such as fear, anger, guilt, orshame*

·   *Loss of interest in previous activities*

·   *Feelings of social isolation*

·   *Difficulty feeling positive emotions, such as happiness orsatisfaction*

Cognition and mood symptoms can begin or worsen after the traumatic event. They can lead people to feel detached from friends or family members.

However, we now realize that the *symptoms of PTSD may not be as straightforward* as we had thought. The disorder appears to be *more complex and may affect more people* who have not been diagnosed with it. The additional symptoms now being considered to be in this diagnosis include "*feelings of worthlessness, shame, and guilt; problems controlling your emotions; finding it hard to feel connected with other people; and relationship problems, like having trouble keeping friends and partners.*"

It goes without saying that anyone who would be involved in a terrifying experience, such as a school shooting or being present in a war zone, being a victim of sexual or child abuse, domestic violence, or having been harmed in some way by someone you trusted might have the disorder. Each instance can implant that **fear and anxiety response** that we have seen in similar situations, however, usually in wartime. We might think of these episodes as a different **type of war** that battles in our brains.

Children are not exempt from this diagnosis, but it may not be accurately applied. It is easy to **mistake the signs** of traumatic stress for those of attention-deficit/hyperactivity disorder (ADHD) in youngsters because both conditions can make affected children seem clumsy and irritable. To avoid excluding experiences of trauma that might be distasteful, interviewers must take care during any health or mental health evaluation. There should be no **age exclusion criteria** in this regard.

Neuroimaging is also pointing to some previously unseen brain implications with PTSD. It is well known that post-traumatic stress disorder (PTSD), which affects both emotion and memory, can have an impact on the cerebellum, a region of the brain that aids in *controlling movement and balance*. Who knows whether a smaller cerebellum makes a person more likely to get post-traumatic stress disorder (PTSD) or *whether PTSD causes the brain region to shrink?*

Various treatments are available for those affected, and new therapies are also being explored to help relieve those with these symptoms since they can be life-changing. No one should suffer needlessly or feel ashamed because they are experiencing these symptoms. They've **been in a battle for their sanity**, and now it is time to heal, and the healers must be available for them.

Chapter 41: A Disorder That Makes Monster Faces Out of Everyone You See

I magine what would happen if suddenly everyone's face that you saw became an unfamiliar and very disturbing one. What would you do and could you tell anyone that this was happening without having them think you were mentally deranged? This particular type of visual distortion does happen, however. People with prosopometamorphosia have a rare eye distortion that changes how they see faces. **Its exact cause is unknown,** but it is generally linked to neurological disorders like migraines, epilepsy, and abnormal findings on CT scans and MRIs of the head. It has also been associated with Epstein-Barr virus.

The British neurologist Macdonald Critchley coined the word prosopometamorphopsia to describe a type of metamorphopsia in which people see people's faces or parts of faces distortedly. On CT studies and MRIs of the head, metamorphoses are often linked to diseases of the eyes or brain.

The disorder should not be confused with another facial recognition issue, prosopagnosia, also known as **face blindness**. In this more common disorder, people are affected in different ways. Some people might not tell the difference between strangers and people they don't know very well. Some people might not recognize their own faces or the faces of their family and friends. The actor, Brad Pitt, has admitted he may have the disorder and frequently cannot recognize people he knows.

Different people have different symptoms that can change the size, shape, color, and placement of facial features. The problem can last days, weeks, or even years, another thing that can change about PMO.

A new study of one person provided us more information about this problem. Faces didn't look twisted to the 58-year-old man with PMO when they were seen on a screen or on paper, but they looked "demonic" when he saw them in person. Why would it only happen when he's with the person? It almost sounds like there's an element of emotion involved. But his wasn't the only case described in the professional literature because one woman with the disorder had an unusual variant of it.

In yet another description of a patient with the disorder, this right-handed 67-year-old woman with a history of coronary artery disease, high cholesterol, high blood pressure, and diabetes mellitus described how she could see people's faces tilted to the left. It seemed like the left eye on people's faces was moving to the side and up when she saw them in person or watched TV pictures of people.

Looking at her own face in the mirror or at pictures of faces didn't cause her to see any distortion. It was no problem for her to recognize faces, and only faces seemed twisted to her. Her neurological test came back normal. Additionally, her eye test did not reveal any significant findings. After two months of showing symptoms, a brain MRI revealed **a brain obstruction or subacute infarct**.

People with **Alice in Wonderland syndrome** (AIWS) can have one of 40 types of metamorphopsia. Any part of the face-processing network can be involved, from the occipital to the frontal lobe. The link between the brain's two hemispheres plays a key role, which suggests it may be because of interhemispheric transfer. There are many reasons for this, such as a stroke, seizure, or migraine. It can change how the whole face is seen. But, curiously, up to 30% of teens have short episodes of AIWS symptoms, according to research. However, the disorder is elusive because of the lack of documentation. Once again, we have a syndrome, but we don't have any conclusive evidence to indicate what precipitates it or how common it might be.

<u>What Are the Diagnostic Criteria for AIWS?</u>

There is also disagreement among experts about the exact symptoms and criteria for the disorder. Currently, there are no agreed-upon criteria for AIWS, so physicians usually use their professional opinion to decide whether someone has it. Because of the lack of consensus, experts think that this condition is often not identified or has an incorrect diagnosis.

Exploring possible causation besides brain dysfunction, there are several other ways the strange perceptual changes can happen. It is possible for AIWS to be a sign of a mental illness or a side effect of many medications. We've seen this in elderly patients with dementia who are taking certain medications for allergies.

While working on an Alzheimer's protocol, I came across a couple where the husband had taken medication for allergies and began insisting that his wife should tell the people in their living room to leave. There were no people in the living room. He was having visual hallucinations brought on by that over-the-counter medication. Another woman, who had recently undergone cataract surgery with a type of anesthesia, began to see worms in a frying pan on her stove. Obviously, there were no worms, and it was a side effect of the medication. This is yet another illustration of how medication's can distort our perception, and they need to be ruled out before any diagnosis can be made. Then there are medications like those found in cough medicines used to treat asthma, and topiramate, which is used to treat seizures. Brain tumors can also cause it.

Could the disorder be caused by a mental illness such as schizophrenia? Delusions and hallucinations are important signs of schizophrenia. However, visual hallucinations and illusions are less likely to be the first signs and are usually associated with substance abuse. Although psychiatrists are taught to ask about hallucinations, most of the time, visual illusions and hallucinations are signs of health problems because auditory hallucinations are more common. But the symptoms vary so much that this adds to the difficulty of diagnosis.

Currently, the professional literature lists 42 visible symptoms and 16 somesthetic and other nonvisual symptoms. Treatments vary according to how the symptoms are viewed and have been treated with various methods, including ECT. Researchers now know that, while AIWS is rare, it may be under-reported because of the lack of diagnostic criteria. However, it appears to be a short-lived perceptual change in many cases.

Anyone experiencing any of these symptoms is advised to consult with a medical professional for evaluation rather than think it will simply go away by itself. Significant, treatable disorders could require medical attention.

Chapter 42: Is Breakfast the Most Important Meal of the Day? Maybe Not.

M any people believe that breakfast is the most important meal of the day. But is it, and what happens if you skip the traditional breakfast? Will you wilt and be sluggish, and will it decrease your ability to be creative or study? And where did the idea originate?

You guessed it: Lobbyists were involved once the idea was offered by Edward Bernays, a nephew of Sigmund Freud who patched together several factors that could be used to create a new interest in breakfast. A physician agreed with Bernays that a heavy breakfast of bacon and eggs was better for you than a light breakfast. The physician then sent this statement to about 5,000 doctors and asked them to sign it. Newspapers reported the petition's results as if they were a scientific study. Bacon and eggs became king as the best breakfast for everyone.

We see the same sort of consumer manipulation in certain pharmaceutical products, where you may note "more hospitals use..." for a certain analgesic. What it really means is that pharmaceutical firms give hospitals free medication to dispense to their patients, so of course, more of them use it. Have you ever thought of that?

Of course, Bernays was one of many involved in efforts to increase the importance of breakfast, and for that, we have to look at John Harvey Kellogg. Kellogg was a physician, and an advocate of the Battle Creek Sanitarium, where some unusual techniques were used to maintain health.

John's brother Keith Kellogg came up with the breakfast food corn flakes. The result, of course, was a fortune in the making. Breakfast cereals then burst on the American scene as the answer to an increasing workforce's need for something quick and nutritious to start the day off. Cereal was later manufactured with additional nutrients, which only increased its allure. After Kellogg's, of course, came other high-profile breakfast cereals, such as the ones created by C. W. Post. The breakfast wars were on.

Statistics show that in 2020, 283.39 million Americans ate cold breakfast foods. In 2024, this number was expected to rise to 290.32 million. Consumption mainly relies on effective advertising in the midst of inconclusive scientific results, so the only thing we know is that the product's marketing and public relations have been successful in finding a robust market.

Even the slogan "Breakfast is the most important meal of the day" was in service of a product that needed to be sold. James Caleb Jackson and John Harvey Kellogg came up with it in the 1800s to promote their new breakfast cereal.

Unfortunately, dinner and lunch were never treated the same, and we still only eat a few types of foods for breakfast and it is still mostly breakfast foods like cereal, bacon and eggs, rolls, bagels, and biscuits. I recall that as a graduate student, I did consume an orange-flavored product called Instant Breakfast before I went to my first morning class, skipping breakfast completely.

A professor I had changed his entire eating schedule around. He had steak, potatoes, vegetables, and toast in the morning. In the evening, instead of a regular dinner, he had yogurt, fruit, and possibly a small salad. By following this eating schedule, he lost nearly 100 pounds. His strategy involved consuming more calories in the morning, which could be burned off throughout the day, than having a larger meal at night. So, for him, breakfast was the most important meal of the day, but it differed from what we usually think of as breakfast.

In recent years, breakfast has been linked to controlling weight, being a cardiometabolic risk factor, and problems with brain function. Although breakfast is commonly seen as essential for a healthy diet, people often ignore the nutritional value of their food.

But is there some science to back up the claims about breakfast and how it ranks in our daily eating schedule? People who are into fitness and health are becoming more interested in intermittent fasting, so you may be wondering if you can go without breakfast. When you do intermittent fasting, you do not have to eat breakfast; you are told not to. Most people do a 16-hour fast overnight, then eat anything they want for 8 hours.

Still, nutritionists have long said that breakfast is very important. Nutritionists at Henry Ford Health say breakfast sets the tone for the day. Is it better to skip breakfast or wait until later? It depends. Patients who are overweight might not be able to eat much, or they may need to reduce the amount of energy they consume. According to research, eating breakfast daily can help us stay alert and focused at work and school. Eating breakfast can also help you feel full and prevent overeating later in the day, which can help maintain your weight.

A new study suggests that adults who skip breakfast are likely to miss out on the most abundant nutrients in the foods that make up morning meals. And skipping breakfast can leave you without important nutrients for the entire day, as in this study of over 30,000 American adults.

Should you skip breakfast? The answer for you depends on a number of things, including the calories you will need in the morning, your weight control issues, as well as health issues, and what type of diet you find most effective for yourself. It would be wonderful if there were one hard-and-fast rule for breakfast, but it appears that there are a number of differing experts and studies that are either pro or con regarding eating breakfast. It's not an easy issue, and it will be debated as long as there are people eating breakfast and breakfast interests providing material to patients and physicians alike.

If the state of medical education is as it was when I was working in public relations for pharmaceutical companies, young medical students receive possibly two hours on diet, and I suspect there is very little on breakfast during those seminars.

Breakfast or not? You decide with the help of your healthcare providers.

Chapter Forty-Three

Chapter 43: VR Forest Bathing Is Beneficial For Mental Health

Research has provided enough information on the health value of "forest bathing," and now we know that it can be done virtually as well. The Japanese ritual of "Shinrin-yoku," which entails immersing yourself in nature to improve your mental and physical well-being, has been modernized as "virtual forest bathing."

With the development of technology, platforms for virtual reality (VR) and augmented reality (AR) now give people the chance to experience the therapeutic benefits of nature without being physically present, making this activity available to everyone, including those with mobility issues or chronic illnesses who are confined to bed. But there are several elements missing here and they include the volatile oils in the air in the forest, the effects of sunshine and the other forest scents that seems to affect us.

Being in a natural forest setting, whether actually walking there or watching it virtually, can elevate mood, lessen negative emotions, and boost positive affect.

The benefits of exposure to nature, even digitally, include the restoration of cognitive function and an increase in attention span. Virtual nature experiences can increase cognitive performance and restore attention, resulting in better concentration and focus. Virtual forest bathing has also shown potential for reducing depression and anxiety symptoms. Researchers discovered in a study that those who participated in virtual nature experiences experienced lower levels of anxiety and despair, indicating the potential therapeutic use of these interventions.

And you don't need to leave your home or office. The accessibility of virtual forest bathing is one of its best features. Those who are physically confined or have limited access to natural settings can interact with nature through virtual experiences. Its openness encourages egalitarianism and broadens the application of nature-based therapies for mental health.

We know forest bathing is beneficial for mental health, and now it is believed the same is true for virtual forest bathing. The advantages include a decrease in stress, improvement of emotional well-being, enhancement of cognitive function, and reduction of depressive and phobic symptoms.

Many scientific investigations and research publications back up these conclusions. Virtual nature experiences also have the potential to be therapeutic tools due to their accessibility and inclusion and can become a crucial component of mental health interventions as technology develops, giving people a practical and efficient way to connect with nature for enhanced well-being.

One difficulty that remains is that people must first have access to virtual reality technology. Typically, this consists of VR headgear (check online for the latest equipment and compare prices), as well as controllers or sensors that work with it. These gadgets produce an engrossing virtual setting that mimics being present in a forest or other natural area. But if cost is a consideration, think about a phone app for forest bathing instead. Once you have the gear, you can choose from a selection of different virtual woodland bathing experiences. Several VR programs and applications have been created expressly to mimic natural settings and offer a peaceful, immersive experience. They are accessible through dedicated VR content producers, platforms like Steam, the Oculus Store, and others.

Many websites, including YouTube, provide top-notch nature videos and 360-degree experiences that can mimic the experience of being in a forest. People can browse these immersive movies and virtually immerse themselves in natural settings by using a computer, tablet, or smartphone. To uncover relevant information, perform a search for "virtual forest bathing" or "360-degree nature experiences."

Several nature apps and websites are available that offer the virtual sensations of taking a woodland bath. These platforms frequently offer a selection of crisp pictures, soothing sounds, and interactive features that let users interact with digital forests. Nature Soundmap and Nature Treks VR are other examples (which also offer a VR option for those with equipment).

There are even guided meditations and mindfulness exercises created to mimic the feelings of being in nature that can also be used to practice virtual forest bathing. People can be led through a virtual journey using audio recordings or mobile applications that are centered on nature-based meditation, which can help people unwind and mentally connect with nature.

In addition, please keep in mind that the forest has several nature sounds, or you can use ambient music, which is another approach to mimic the sensation of taking a forest bath. Birdsong, rustling leaves, and flowing water are just a few of the peaceful nature sounds that can be found on several websites and smartphone apps. Such sounds can evoke a sense of being in the outdoors and can create an immersive audio atmosphere.

Last but not least, people can experience virtual woodland bathing by using their imagination and vision abilities. Shut your eyes, go somewhere peaceful, and imagine yourself in a tranquil forest. As you imagine the sights, sounds, and smells of the forest, pay attention to the minute details and feelings associated with being in nature. Even without external stimuli, this practice can still be beneficial for the mind and the soul. The technique is, in fact, a form of self-hypnosis.

Just keep in mind that while these techniques deliver virtual experiences, they might not provide the same level of immersion as VR technology. Yet, by developing an emotional and mental connection with nature, people can still improve their ability to unwind, reduce stress, and generally feel good.

Apps for "forest bathing" that provide immersive outdoor experiences:

Meta Quest2 and HTC Vive are only a couple of the VR platforms that support the app Nature Treks VR. It offers users access to virtual forests, mountains, and waterfalls so they can explore and become completely engrossed in serene natural settings.

For iOS smartphones, the app store may be one place you can find what you want. Users of these apps can virtually travel through beautiful forests and feel the calming effects of nature thanks to the visuals and tranquilizing sounds they offer.

Google Earth VR (only for Windows): The Google Earth platform has been converted to work in virtual reality. Users can virtually travel to forests and natural landscapes from all over the world, offering a sense of being there in various natural areas while also providing a worldwide exploration experience.

Please be aware that depending on the device or platform, availability and compatibility may change. It is advised to check the relevant app stores or platforms for the most recent information and device compatibility.

Chapter 44: Are Healing Sounds the New Way to Anxiety and Stress Relief?

Sound is all around us. Most of it we hear, but many of them we either don't hear or unconsciously block out to make ourselves less stimulated by them. In fact, we still have muscles in our ears that some people have the ability to use to a greater degree than the rest of us. How do people use these muscles? Have you ever heard of ear wiggling? I wrote an article on this on medium.com, and you might want to go there and read it. What it indicates is that we do have the ability to shut down some of the noise coming into our ears by utilizing these muscles, almost unconsciously.

I know that, while I was waiting on a platform for a subway train, the train would come into the station making screeching noises, and without touching my ears, I could shut down some of that noise with those wonderful little muscles. Yes, I am one of those people who have this ability. In fact, I showed my undergraduate class how I could wiggle my ears, and they were astonished. Of course, it's not anything like a dog or a cat can do, but the subtle little changes are helpful in harsh environments.

On a different level, for thousands of years, Tibetan and Buddhist communities have embraced singing bowl sound meditation as a traditional technique *to promote healing and relaxation*. For the purpose of producing a therapeutic auditory experience, the technique requires the skillful *employment of bowls*, which are often constructed of a variety of materials such as crystal or brass.

These bowls have been purposefully crafted to provide a sound that is both resonant and soothing when they are hammered or struck with a mallet. When the bowls are struck, they produce harmonic tones and vibrations that can go deep into the body, and it is believed they can affect the body's energy system (energetic system).

There are a variety of advantages that have been associated with the practice of employing singing bowls in sound healing meditation. These advantages include a *reduction in stress and anxiety, a decrease in heart rate and blood pressure, and an improvement in spiritual welfare*. The precise mechanisms that are responsible for these effects are not completely understood; nevertheless, it is possible that they entail alterations in differences in brain waves.

An observational investigation was aimed to uncovering the potential effects of singing bowl meditation on mood, stress, anxiety, physical pain, and spiritual well-being. A substantial difference was discovered in response to all of the endpoints. In particular, a tension subscale had extremely significant effects on the participants after they had completed the meditation exercises. This lends credence to the hypothesis that sound meditation would *increase feelings of relaxation* and decrease *feelings of stress.*

When compared to the ratings obtained before meditation, the scores for *anxiety and negative mood were significantly lower* after receiving meditation. The results of the meditation showed that less-desired *mood states, such as tension, anger, and despair, were reduced after the meditation. In contrast,* potentially positive factors increased, such as a sense of spiritual well-being.

In addition to singing bowls, there is another variant called singing bowl massage, where the bowls are *placed on the individual's body.* A study of this kind found that applying a singing bowl massage is beneficial physically and psychologically.

To answer whether the effects are also therapeutic, researchers evaluated the effects of singing bowl massage on patients experiencing chronic *pain* that was not specific to any particular area. Due to the limited number of studies that were qualified for inclusion, a recent evaluation concluded that additional data is needed before singing bowl therapies may be recommended.

The research goes on. Another study investigated the effect of striking a singing bowl *on the level of tiredness experienced during the day.* The singing bowl was used to induce a state of relaxation that considerably reduced subjective tiredness. The difference was still considerable in women even when gender stratification was taken into account.

What should we take away from this research? Utilizing the soothing sounds of Tibetan singing bowl (TSB) sound-based treatment is an exemplary supplemental treatment that shows great potential.

Composed of metal alloys, a continuous and soothing sound is produced by base tone results that combine with a sequence of overtones.

Evidence suggests that TSB can elicit improvements in distress, anxiety, sadness, weariness, and tension, as well as in blood pressure, *heart rate, respiratory rate, peripheral capillary oxygen saturation, cutaneous conductance, and alpha power as evaluated by electroencephalography*. But is this more a function of the individual's belief that the bowl therapy will work? It could be.

Music and music therapy have found their place in treatments for both physical and mental disorders; we might also include Tibetan singing bowls.

Chapter 45: You Can Change Those Medical Consent Forms

I n healthcare, informed consent means patients know the risks and benefits of medical procedures beforehand. Consent forms are key in detailing the procedure's specifics, potential risks, and patient rights. Patients may sometimes want to exclude specific items from these forms, such as video recording, photography, or future use of their information by healthcare providers. This article indicates how patients can customize consent forms to safeguard their privacy and independence. It also covers factors such as consent form validity and duration.

how many times during or before a medical procedure have you been presented with a form and simply asked to sign it? Were you given adequate time to read the entire form, or were you rushed through it and reassured that it really was just procedure?

Understanding Medical Consent Forms

Medical consent forms provide information about a medical procedure or treatment, including its risks, benefits, and other options. They prove that the patient has been properly informed and consented to the procedure. However, patients may change these forms according to their needs and concerns. There is no mandate that you sign the form as it is. Unfortunately, sometimes the form is handed to you in a stack and not singled out as a medical consent form, and you are just asked to sign everything. This is not the way things are supposed to be handled.

I once stood in the hallway at a major New York City hospital and saw an elderly man, seated alone in a hospital gown on a bed. Beside him, with a clipboard in hand, was a young woman in a white coat urging him to sign a form, which she was not explaining to him. He said he did not have his glasses, and she reassured him that it was OK if he just signed the form. Was that OK? It most certainly was not. He was waiting for a procedure, and she was pushing him to sign a form without him knowing anything about what the form contained. It was a total lack of respect for that man and for her ethical responsibility toward a patient.

Editing Consent Forms

Patients can remove certain parts of a medical consent form by clearly stating their preferences. They can cross out or delete the sections they don't agree with or add a note explaining the changes they want, plus, **date and initial** the portion that is struck out of the original consent form. Patients must clearly express their preferences and ensure the updated form accurately reflects their wishes.

Legal Considerations

When changing medical consent forms, patients must consider the legal aspects involved. Healthcare providers may decline a procedure if they believe the changes made by the patient could affect the quality of care or their safety. Patients need to understand that altering a consent form might limit their options if something goes wrong during the procedure. For example, if you delete the part about videotaping, you might need such evidence in the future if there is an issue. Also understand that consent forms have a life and each state may have a different period of time during which the consent form is active. Usually, it would be about 3 to 6 months. Certainly, a consent form does not go for a year or more, and a new form must be requested after the specified expiration of the current form.

Validity and Duration of Consent Forms

The validity and duration of medical consent forms can vary based on the specific situation. Typically, these forms are valid for the duration of the treatment or procedure they were meant for. Remember, there might be exceptions, such as if the patient's condition changes significantly or if new information about the procedure comes up.

Yes, it's important to consider all aspects and for patients to consider the consequences of changing consent forms. But also, don't be rushed into not reading the form completely because they are waiting for you in the procedure room. You could sign to be included in a research protocol that is not your intention. One instance of where a consent form wasn't even presented to a patient (who died in 1952 from cervical cancer) before her cancer cells were harvested was that of **Henrietta Lacks**. Details are in the book *"The Immortal Life of Henrietta Lacks"* by Rebecca Skloot.

After harvesting Ms. Lacks cancer cells, the researcher then went on to make millions by signing licensing agreements for their use ("HeLa" cells) in clinical trials all over the world. Only after the family, many years after her death, became aware of this ruse, did they institute a legal action. Because the details of the settlement were to remain secret, the Henrietta Lacks family did not get any money from the deal with Thermo Fisher Scientific. A lawsuit that had been brought in 2021 was finally settled.

She was not the only one from whom tissue was taken and then used in far-flung research for which the original researcher was paid. Can you say greedy and unethical? Of course you can. Other, less well-known cases involved, at least one man who, over a period of at least two years, made regular trips to a research facility where they removed material from his body that was then used in research projects.

The Supreme Court of California decided that medical professionals could obtain samples and fluids from cancer patient **John L. Moore** for research, but **he did not have any ownership rights to them.** Again, his material was licensed and used, and the school (Regents of the University of California) received a great deal of money from it. Moore established a precedent in California that states **individuals do not have any property rights to bodily samples taken by their doctors**, even though doctors are supposed to tell patients about their research interests. Moore gave his OK to a spleen removal procedure, but he was vague about the research goals and did not give his explicit permission to use his cells in the study. The court, nevertheless, found that it was in the best interest of research to proceed to use Moore's spleen cells for research. By the year 1990, Moore's cells had a **potential market value of $3.01 billions.**

Of course, one of the most disastrous, unethical, and horrendous bits of medical research history was one in which the individuals, Black men in the South in the US, were deceived regarding the direction of a research project. What was it? **The Untreated Syphilis Study at Tuskegee** was an experiment that ran from 1932 to 1972 and was funded by the United States Public Health Service (USPHS). Untreated syphilis was supposed to be the subject of the study's natural history component. Researchers did not get participants' informed consent because it was not a requirement of the study. The men never knew that they had active syphilis, and would develop dementia and die, and were not receiving any treatment for it. Even after penicillin was readily available, the subjects were still not given any of the available medicines.

How much did the men who participated in the study get out of the settlement that happened in 1974? There were four parts to the $10 million payout:

> 1. Everyone who took part in the living syphilitic group got $37,500.

> 2. The syphilitic group gave $15,000 to the heirs of those who died while participating.

> 3. Each participant in the living control group received $16,000.

> 4. The heirs of those who died while in the control group got $5,000.

During the 1950s, when government agencies were interested in a form of mind control with **LSD,** researchers managed to deliver this drug to college students in New York City and other colleges. The students were never told that they were part of a clandestine operation for the intelligence units in the government, and we do not know if any of them suffered lasting effects from it. Even if they were given a consent form, because it was intelligence in nature, it is a safe assumption that they were not given appropriate details regarding the potential dangers of LSD and how it could affect their lives. Well, some may believe that there is benefit to LSD, I recall being in a premed biology course during my freshman year at college. One of the students in our group suddenly disappeared, and when we inquired, we were told he had taken a quantity of LSD and had to be admitted to a psychiatric hospital. He never came back to school.

These are only three egregious examples of research projects. There are probably many more of which we are unaware, and it underscores the need for people to be thoroughly briefed on any procedure, medical or otherwise, so that they know what they are getting into. Often, however, the details may be somewhat massaged in order to encourage people to be participants.

Chapter Forty-Six

Chapter 46: Denials of Disability Benefits Are Not Always About the Rules

As disabled workers, disabled widows or widowers, or handicapped adult children, 9,243,999 persons were receiving Social Security disability benefits as of December 2021. About 85.2 percent of the participants were disabled workers, 12.4 percent were adult children with disabilities, and 2.4 percent were widows or widowers with disabilities.

A listing of all of the psychological claims categories currently found in the Social Security disability manuals is covered in a book I wrote years ago that is available on Amazon (*A Social Security Disabil-*

ity Psychological Claims Handbook:: A simple guide to understanding your SSD claim for psychological impairments and unraveling the maze of decision making) in paperback.

Many times, people approach Social Security Disability applications for psychological or mental problems with tremendous anxiety and concern because they see this as an arduous process. The worries I have encountered when talking to people I have advised to apply for benefits range from thinking they will face something more stressful than not having enough money to cover their everyday expenses to thinking they will be turned down (and humiliated) to a real fear of the examiner and what they will have to go through.

Some medical professionals perform benefits analyses for applicants where the evaluator has a personal or political agenda that they utilize in this work. This leads to many people being denied when they should have been allowed, and it is in everyone's best interest to **ask for reconsideration** or use other means to obtain their justifiable benefits.

I have seen this happen with many cases of women who had MS or persons with Lyme disease where the physician refused to recognize the disability of that individual. A major newspaper in California once contacted me to ask for an opinion on a physician doing evaluations who claimed he could do 60 in one hour. I think the only way he could have done that was to deny all of them without even reading the report. Some medical consultants will deny benefits outright to increase their income in states where they are paid per case rather than per hour.

The current situation in Great Britain has raised how often denials of benefits for disabled people are made there. The UK government denies more than 40% of disability benefit requests from people with multiple sclerosis (MS), cerebral palsy, and arthritis. One in four applications from amputees is also turned down. Unfortunately, details on how many people with psychological disorders are turned down are not available. For these individuals, there is a group called Fightback4Justice.

In the United States, applicants must rely on reports from their medical professionals, reconsideration of their case, specialized attorneys, or their US Senator's office (called a "**sensitive inquiry**"). These Congressional offices have someone who will handle disability benefits cases for claimants who contact them. This feature is a means to have your case either reevaluated and not left to languish without a speedy response. Use it because it is there for you.

Your claim is not over after a denial. As I've indicated above, you have options if your claim is turned down and what you can do if it seems to be taking a long time to resolve.

Regretfully, many people also think they are not disabled enough to get benefits or that they can't handle the process. For some, having to acknowledge that they are incapacitated for whatever reason is a personal insult, or they feel shame. These people view psychiatrists and psychologists as unsettling professionals who will probe their thoughts and inflict even more suffering.

Anyone can have an evaluation from their own psychologist or psychiatrist, who should **never use the words "this person is permanently disabled"** in their report. That sentence is meaningless to Social Security Disability and will be useless in any application process.

Basically, what disability wants to know is whether or not you can maintain something called PPC—pace, persistence, and concentration at a task without constant supervision. There are also stipulations about the amount of weight that someone may be able to lift or carry. Medical schools do not prepare anyone for this type of indication. Therefore, weight should be eliminated and can be seen as a reason for denial.

Remember that people's work histories and a fund they have contributed to have financed the benefits. **Social Security is not an entitlement**; it is something you pay for. Now, you might have to defend taking part of the benefits money early. This is not charity or a handout. Recall that always. Never forget, either, that you are to be treated with deference and politeness.

Disproving or proving claims of mental health impairments can be more challenging than those of physical impairments. For this reason, resolving the claim depends on being aware of the procedure, which emphasizes getting sufficient records from all healthcare professionals. This would speed up the process and maybe spare you from sitting for a Consultative Exam (CE).

Anyone administering a CE will use the Green Book (online) for guidance. Remember that anyone performing a CE exam has never seen you before and is **acting on that one meeting alone.**

Once benefits are approved, an individual may be put on a schedule for reevaluation (one year, three years, seven years), or maybe "medical improvement not expected" or known in the agency as a MINE case.

There are also types of claims that will always be paid because of the nature of the impairment. For example, claims from people who have severe cognitive impairment due to Alzheimer's, brain damage, head injuries, some genetic disorders that cause psychiatric disorders, and other conditions. People in hospitals or other supervised places will probably keep their pay status. However, people working at their facilities will need to provide reports to them.

Yes, applying for any type of disability benefit may seem stressful, but they can be applied for online now, and it's not always necessary to go to a specific disability office. If you are disabled, either for a short time or more than one year, or have a terminal illness, please use the benefits to which you are entitled. If you are denied and even denied at a reconsideration hearing, **contact one of the larger, national legal companies that represent disability cases**. I referred someone to one, and not only did he receive benefits, he got two years more than he expected.

Also of note is that disability regards anyone over the age of 50 as being "unemployable" because companies usually hire younger workers at lower wages. This can also be a point in favor of anyone applying for benefits. For additional information on psychological disability, please refer to my book, as I've indicated,, "*A Social Security Disability Psychological Claims Handbook:: A simple guide to understanding your SSD claim for psychological impairments and unraveling the maze of decision making*," on Amazon. I have also written another Disability book for children's claims ("*A Social Security Disability Psychological Claims Guidebook for Children's Benefits*") and you may want to review that one, too. It is also on Amazon in paperback form.

Several things you also have in your favor when you apply for disability benefits include 1. **advanced age** (50 or over), 2. a **history of psychiatric or psychological treatment** (including medication if appropriate), **3. inability to have worked for several years**, and 4. **medical illnesses**, such as diabetes, heart, disease, or any other medical illness. All of them are included in the consideration for your application. As a former medical consultant for Disability, I know that these four things would strengthen your case for a rating of 03, which would provide you with benefits.

Chapter 47: Spirituality Has a Role in Treatment, and Healthcare Now Realizes It

A sense of purpose forms the foundation for life, and in medicine, spirituality has long been neglected as a necessary or even incidental part of treatment. Not seen as anchored to specific religions, attention is now being paid to how powerful a role spirituality can play, just as pharmaceutical and surgical interventions do. New research points toward a sense of spirituality, lending treatment options or extensions for cancer patients.

According to some studies, spiritual and religious practices may help people maintain a positive attitude. This can make both patients and guardians feel better. Being spiritually or religiously healthy helps patients feel less anger and discomfort. It can also cut down on drug and alcohol abuse. It might lower the risk of heart disease and high blood pressure. Spiritual health may also help them feel more at peace and guilt-free.

How do we find spirituality, especially if we wish to divorce it from standardized, established religions? A feeling of oneness and connection to others, a higher power, or the natural world are common ways to describe spiritual experiences. A feeling of purpose and meaning in life is often linked to spirituality. This also shows connections. Spiritual "unhealth" could mean being *disconnected, feeling alone, unmoored, or without hope*. This sense of disconnection often leads to depression and may, perhaps, account for the worldwide *sense of loneliness* that is being seen as an epidemic. How can we remediate this? One way is to recognize the relevance of a sense of connection or spirituality and proceed from there.

Human relationships can show signs of spiritual disconnect. For example, most of us felt alone during the COVID-19 pandemic, and the U.S. Surgeon General has called the present "epidemic" of loneliness an alarming problem. The way we relate to nature can also show signs of spiritual disconnect. Our world's instability is having a bigger effect on people, but they may feel helpless to make a difference. Tribal groups like American Indians, Alaska Natives, and Canadian First Nations may not experience this disconnectedness or loneliness because they have strong ties to nature.

Many medical ethicists agree that doctors need to do more than just fix the details of patients' physical and mental problems in order to follow the principles of beneficence and care for them as whole persons. Spirituality and religion are important to many patients.

When patients get sick, get better, or die, they and their families go through it all as whole people. Ignoring the spiritual parts of their lives and identities is not respectful, and it cuts medical practice off from the basic way that patients feel and deal with their problems. To help patients, you need to pay attention to what they think is best. If you want to treat patients like people, you have to **pay attention to their moral needs.**

Leading medical and public health publications have put together special issues on the topic of spirituality and medicine. A growing trove of strong, empirical research connects spiritual beliefs, states of being, group practices, and private rituals to many health benefits, such as a lower risk of death from all causes.

Some experts in public health have named faith and spirituality "determinants of health.". Additionally, the COVID-19 pandemic brought to light the unique health benefits of receiving religious and spiritual support. The World Health Organization (WHO) highlighted a new wave of collaboration with faith-based groups and the important roles faith communities play as public health leaders. For example, many faith communities promote safety measures like masks and vaccines.

<u>Practicing Spirituality</u>

How do individuals practice their spirituality, and how do healthcare professionals acknowledge it? Spirituality, not aligned with organized religion, is a sense of internal purpose and peace. It arises from a desire to make life meaningful for as long as we are alive and from a belief that we have a soul or some connection with a supernatural being or natural force.

Spirituality is the search for something holy, while religion is a set of organized or shared ideas and practices. That can be a higher power or other things in life, like loving relationships, nature, or work. It can happen inside or outside of a religious practice. Many people in the U.S. say they are spiritual but not religious. The number of people responding to current surveys indicates that more people are leaving organized religion but still identifying themselves as spiritual.

In a dramatically changing world, we will see new alliances being formed, which will permit individual beliefs to meld with societal needs, resulting in a strong sense of purpose, whether believing in God or not. Faith-based and nonreligious civic actors can work together in new ways, especially at the neighborhood level. These kinds of relationships help people who are homeless and others around the world adjust to climate change.

A timely study from the World Economic Forum also lists examples of how business and religious groups have worked together. Some CRCC friends and "spiritual exemplars" are among these people. The stories of those who promote this type of new spirituality are there for the reading.

Healthcare is also catching up, and some medical schools are beginning to offer courses specifically to train physicians to be more engaged with patients who express a sense of spirituality and to provide them with treatment opportunities. Psychologists are also being trained by professional organizations to include spirituality in psychotherapy and to gain a deeper understanding of patients and their needs in this area.

Times are changing, and the dramatic physical changes worldwide in terms of climate, culture, and corporate involvement are all promoting a new spirituality that can only result in a sense of closeness, even for those who are far from us. But in hospitals and offices, too, there needs to be an appreciation and understanding of individual forms of spirituality without resorting to diagnostic labeling.

Chapter 48: Research Has a Blind Eye When It Comes to Women

The question for healthcare must be: how can you prescribe when you don't have relevant research to support what you're doing? It may seem rather parochial to ask this question, but it is highly relevant since analysis of research studies over the past several decades indicates that women have been underrepresented in clinical trials.

In an analysis of 1433 trials with 302,664 subjects, 41.2% were women on average. Women were underrepresented in cardiovascular disease studies compared to the number of women with the disease

(49% of people with cardiovascular disease are women). Women comprise 60% of psychiatry patients, and 42.0% of people who participated in clinical studies were women. Also, only 41.0% of people who took part in cancer clinical studies were women, even though 51% of cancer patients are women.

The seriousness of this lack of inclusion was addressed by the NIH Revitalization Act of 1993 Public Law 103–43, which stated in Section 492A, that women and minorities should be included in clinical research.

Even though this was in place in 1993, and we are now three decades away from this mandate, there is still a paucity of women being included in clinical trials. When we consider that some of the issues being researched pertain more to women than to men, we have to question how their exclusion can be accepted.

And it's not always clinical trials where women and their participation have been absent. When I interviewed him over the phone, Stanley Milgram, who wrote "Obedience to Authority," was miffed when I asked what happened to the women's data in his study.

As I recall, he hung up on me. During the study in which a person was to give an electric shock to someone who was to learn a series of words, women were reluctant to do this. In his book, Milgram admitted he dropped their data because it was insufficient. Perhaps he didn't say exactly "insufficient," but words of that effect. Women, it seems, don't want to cause pain to anyone else, even when it was in a research study.

I think he dropped women's data because it didn't fit his hypothesis about how authoritarian personalities could engage citizens in such activities. Of course, the whole idea came out of the Nazi war trials and the research by Frankel-Brunswick on the authoritarian personality. At that time, researchers were searching for answers to the cruelty that was rampant in Germany and in the Nazi party, and they wanted to see if there were personality characteristics that resulted in this behavior. How can anyone drop women out of this type of study since we know that women were involved in the cruelty in the concentration camps, and, if you want an example, watch the film ("Seven Beauties"). I recall meeting a woman who told me she had worked in the French resistance during World War II and admitted that they freely killed the enemy without feeling. She was a delightful lady who had survived and done well when she came to the United States, even writing a book about her experiences and attending school assemblies where she related her experiences. I remember her saying, "Yes, we shot them and then we made love."

The Problem with Research

Although women make up almost half of the world's population and have been more numerous than men in the US since 1946, researchers have always thought that women's bodies were not typical and men's bodies were the "norm." Even though policy and social changes in the 1990s helped turn things around, women are still usually grossly underrepresented in studies.

Buying and housing both male and female mice is more expensive, and some medical experts do not even use female mice for studies because they fear that the changing hormones and reproductive systems of female mice will mess up the results. But biological differences are highly important.

Studies with females have shown big differences in basic biological processes like how pain is experienced and processed. The lack of pre-clinical research on women has undoubtedly led to worse treatment results for women in this regard.

Pregnancy is often a reason why women cannot take part in clinical trials for medicines. As a result, physicians and nurses often have to assist their patients in deciding what treatment to take with a paucity of information. It may even be harder to determine if the pregnant woman has a serious health problem or a condition connected to pregnancy that needs treatment.

And there is another major area of concern. Healthcare professionals often think that women are less likely to get cardiovascular disease (CVD), even though it kills more women than men every year and is still the top cause of death in women. Women with CAD are more likely to delay or try to avoid or treat their condition because they think estrogen protects them more than men.

The issue is particularly important in cardiac surgery with women. After a CABG, women have a higher rate of operative mortality and morbidity than men. This difference has stayed the same over time, even though heart surgery has changed and improved.

The main reason for this issue has not been figured out yet, even though a lot of studies have been done on baseline patient characteristics and comorbidities, the natural history of CAD in women, differences between men and women in surgical technique, and the possible effects of profound hemodilution and anemia. However, one aspect is that women's cardiac vessels are not the same in diameter as men's, and **most training isn't completed with many female patients.**

There are thoughts about factors during surgery, like the fact that women's coronary arteries are smaller and more reactive, the level of hemodilution anemia during surgery, the type of grafts used, and how well the blood flow is restored, which may play a part.

The facts are irrefutable, and research is mandated to include females in all studies unless serious contraindications indicate otherwise. To treat without research backing the treatment is patently unacceptable and highly questionable.

Chapter 49: Decisions and Mental Health Arise From Your Gut, Not Your Head

W ho would think that your gut plays a pivotal role in your decision-making? It seems so highly improbable, and yet research is pointing in that direction as it explores the intricate connections between the gut and the brain, and the results are astonishing.

There is increasing evidence that the gut microbiome controls social and emotional behavior in both animals and people. However, we still do not know if and how the gut bacteria might affect how people make health decisions in a social setting. New findings in that direction show that an experimental intervention made people more willing to give up a financial reward when they thought they were being treated badly.

This change in how people made social decisions was linked to changes in the amount of tyrosine in their blood when fasting. This suggests that there may be a link between gut bacteria and behavior. The findings help us learn more about how the body and brain work together to make social decisions and why people sometimes act in ways that make little sense from an economic point of view. When considered in this manner, we begin to see how diet and medication can affect our cognitive functioning.

Overall, new stress is now on how important microbiome science is, especially gut microbiota, as new key players in mental disorders and mental health maintenance. The mental health community should welcome this new area of biological psychiatry and postgenomic medicine because it will have a huge impact on integrative and holistic health studies over the next decades.

So, can it be as simple as eating pickles or foods prepared in that manner to protect our gut, especially after taking an antibiotic? Perhaps it is important and foods such as pickles, yogurt and kimchi can be integral parts of health maintenance as well as playing a role in dietary elements that assist mental health. We know antibiotics can wreak havoc on the gut microbiota, and it must be assisted with diet, and the simple addition of food ingredients may be essential.

Foods give our bodies the nutrients they need and also provide food for the gut microbiome, which is the mutualistic microbial flora that lives in our digestive system. Different metabolites are made from parts of food that have not been processed yet. What we eat affects the gut microbiome's structure, makeup, and function. This microbiome works with the gut epithelial and mucosal **immune systems** to keep intestinal homeostasis healthy. But it does much more than affect immune system stability.

Some things that are known to be part of the depressed trait are affected by microbiota. These include an overactive stress response and inflammatory features. Also, the fact that microbiota affects brain growth and changes how people act in social situations makes it possible that it plays a part in autism spectrum disorder and schizophrenia. If changes to microbiota are linked to psychiatric illnesses, then eating probiotics (live bacteria) could help restore the balance of microbiota in the gut, which could have antidepressant or antipsychotic effects.

New research shows a much stronger link between "feeling good" (emotional health) and the health of the gut microbiota community. Changes in gut microbiomes were discovered in many mental illnesses, like schizophrenia, anxiety, depression, and autism spectrum disorder. The microbiota diversity index is one of the most important factors for gut health because it shows how stable and resilient the ecosystem is.

We are biological beings, and evolution has provided us with a highly integrated and interrelated system that works when it is provided for in a specific manner. One of them is diet. It can't be denied its importance, and dietary science will soon become more of a factor in psychiatry and psychology.

Prescriptions for specific foods should be considered just as prescriptions for medications are written; we cannot deny this much-needed change in medicine. There's too much evidence for its inclusion, and future discoveries will only enhance its position in health and behavior.

Chapter 50: How Fast You Eat and When You Eat Affects Health in the Long Term

Weight and diet are two things on many people's minds, and the healthcare field is especially concerned with trying to find ways to help keep weight down to prevent physical illness.

Being overweight is a major problem for health around the world, especially because it raises health risks. Several strategies have been proposed to combat weight gain. In the past ten years, it has been suggested that the rate and regularity of eating may be linked to obesity. Many of us, by this time, are familiar with the famous hot dog eating contest that we have seen, and the fact that there are people who enter competitions where they consume vast amounts of food within a specific short period of time. Competitive eating is what it's called, but we have to wonder if some people are engaging in a type of competitive eating without competing with anyone. I'm speaking, of course, about those who wolf down their food rather than eating at a leisurely pace. The pace at which we eat is now on the table for consideration.

Research has linked fast eating to the risk of being overweight in general, but not enough research has been done on the link between eating quickly and belly fat, which may be even more dangerous to health than overall obesity. Why so much emphasis on belly fat? And how might belly fat be measured? Some would say it's as simple as taking a tape measure to your waistline and seeing what size it registers. But there's two types of fats and one is of concern more than the other.

Having too much fat is bad for your health no matter what shape your body is. But swollen bellies and saddlebags are not the same thing. **Location is important** with body fat, and each year, we learn more about how dangerous fat deep in the belly is compared to the fat that you can pinch with your fingers. One extremely important finding has revealed why this fat is so dangerous to health.

Being aware that **fat cells are endocrine organs** that release hormones and other chemicals that affect other tissues is one of the most important things to happen since the mid-1990s.

Visceral fat was a major risk because it changed the production of cholesterol by letting free fatty acids into the bloodstream and liver. The story has a lot more to it now that we know it. Researchers have found a surprising number of chemicals that connect abdominal fat to many illnesses. So, simply eating quickly carries additional dangers, especially when you eat without hunger.

A previous review of the medical literature from June to September 2020 suggested that kids and adults who eat quickly may be more likely to become overweight. On the other hand, people who eat more often may lose weight and have a lower risk of developing metabolic syndrome. And there's something more here than simply eating fast: hedonic hunger.

When someone is preoccupied with and **wants to eat food for pleasure** rather than because they are physically hungry, this is called **"hedonic hunger."** This idea was given a number value in 2009, when the Power of Food Scale (PFS) was created. The PFS has been used in published studies to predict neural, cognitive, behavioral, anthropometric, and clinical outcomes linked to appetite.

> 1. More hedonic hunger is felt by people younger than 45 and by people who think they are overweight.

2. The self-esteem score decreases as the hedonic hunger number increases.

3. The weight self-stigmatization score increases as the hedonic hunger score increases.

To deal with the hedonic hunger that leads to obesity and to stop the shame and low self-esteem that people who are overweight or obese experience because of their weight, we need effective treatments.

Almost all food intake is done voluntarily. Also, being hungry makes the pleasure of eating even greater. But people often eat even when they do not need calories. This is especially true in modern societies, where tasty foods are everywhere. The extra weight that comes from eating calorie-dense foods that do not need to be eaten is closely linked to the development of diet-related diseases like type II diabetes, heart disease, and high blood pressure.

Many things, like food ads, the smell of food, bad feelings, and watching other people eat, can make someone eat. But what drives this behavior is the pleasure food gives, which can come from positive or negative reinforcement. I recall working for a supermarket magazine once when I learned how supermarket bakeries install an exhaust fan out through the front window so that the baked goods scents hit the consumer before they even enter the store. It was a way of driving traffic to the in-store bakery.

<u>Fast Eaters Slowing Down Tips</u>

How do you begin to change how you eat to eat healthier and, in the process, maintain your health?

1. Twenty to thirty minutes is how long it takes to finish a normal-sized meal. That is how long it takes your body to tell your brain you are full. If you eat quickly, you will eat more in 20 minutes than if you eat slowly.

2. If a fast eater feels full, it is too late; they have already eaten too much and are uncomfortable.

3. Chew your food well enough. Some people feel like their food is sticking to their teeth if they do not chew their food well enough.

4. Take breaks between bites. It is also important to let your stomach and brain rest between bites.

5. Eliminating distractions such as TV, computers, and phones—perhaps even eating in silence.

6. Taking note of how food feels, tastes, and smells.

7. Begin to appreciate the look of the food you're eating.

Is eating too fast and mindlessly bad for you? There's no question about it. Slowing down is not only important for maintaining physical health; it can also improve mental health stability.

Food can be a time for not only eating but also socializing, considering your day, or even kicking back and letting the world go by for a bit. It's a respite time, not rushing to finish and get on with something else.

Your body is not made to rush in terms of how it handles food, and neither is your mind. Give both of them a break.

Chapter 51: Sneezing Has Both a Medical and Religious Connection That Persists to This Day

Anything that bothers the nerve ends in the mucous membranes of the sinuses can cause sneezing, which is called sternutation. When the skin gets irritated, it sends signals to the brain stem. The brainstem controls many of the body's basic processes, such as breathing.

After that, the brain tells the body to move immediately. As the body inhales hard, the glottis, a slit-like opening between the vocal cords, snaps shut. The eyes close, and the body contracts. After that comes the "achoo," a strong exhale that has to go up through the nose because the glottis is closed. The exhale gets rid of the irritants.

A sneeze can send out up to 40,000 droplets, many of which are full of germs and viruses. The droplets move at speeds ranging from 100 to 600 miles per hour. That is a quick and dirty way to do it.

Sneezing is a natural response to an irritant in the environment or, perhaps, a cold you might have. When someone sneezes, you notice that in many cultures, there is an automatic response to people surrounding that person, and the response is, "God bless you." What would be the reason that you would have to give that person a blessing, or have you never thought about it? It has an interesting history that carries over to today as a courtesy, devoid of its origin.

The ancient Romans and Greeks believed that sneezing was a good way to maintain health and expel evil spirits. If we consider viruses evil spirits, that would be OK today. But they weren't the only ones to have this belief, and it was carried over into the Middle Ages, where sneezing might show that someone might have been exposed to the plague, and it would be best to leave their company quickly. Imagine everybody running away when you sneezed. It doesn't sound reasonable.

If the bubonic plague (see Poe's story, "The Masque of the Red Death") were running rampant in Europe, wouldn't it make sense not to be around people who were sneezing? Some, not wanting to worry about sneezers, bolted the door against anyone who wished to come into their home and thought that they could, by that action, seal themselves off from the plague.

One religious leader, Pope Gregory, is most often quoted as encouraging people to offer this brief prayer for the sneezer's health. However, it was still believed that evil forces might attempt to take hold of one's soul, and a sneeze was a way of guarding against this.

In addition to evil forces attempting to take over someone's soul, the belief was that the soul might leave the body during the sneeze or that the person would be vulnerable for an evil spirit to enter. There are, of course, different variations for the languages of the world, but they basically all mean the same thing.

Medicine has had its own view of sneezing. Hippocrates, often seen as the father of modern medicine, indicated that sneezing was a way to expel harmful substances from the lungs. However, there is another belief, or rather a myth, that has held for quite some time. Some people think that the heart stops momentarily during a sneeze and that it is dangerous.

The heart does not stop during sneezing but may make some slight adjustments very briefly due to the change in pressure in our chest. However, it maintains its normal electrical activity, and there is no danger, medically, in sneezing.

Sneezing serves many purposes, and one of them is to clear the nose; another is to act as a warning, either to us or to those around us, that we may be coming down with a virus.

Medical professionals have taught us that the best thing to do when you're going to sneeze is to ensure that you **sneeze into your elbow** and not allow it to release all of those droplets into the air. Children, in particular, should be taught to sneeze into their elbows. It sounds like such a simple thing to do, and yet many people fail to take this precaution.

Chapter 52: The Power in Your Hands and the Amazing Brain Health Connection

B rain research on creativity is based on some false assumptions that almost everyone has. Strangely, this is not a point of contention; once it is made clear, it is easy to see that these assumptions are wrong. Psychology says creativity comprises many complicated mental and emotional processes in discretely different areas.

We treat creativity as a single, unified, and discrete thing, like Einstein had it. As a simple extension of this mistake, cognitive neuroscientists have looked for a type of creative thinking that differs from all other types and has its own brain basis.

So far, research has shown that using neuroscience tools to examine the strength of brain network links can help predict how creative a person will be. But we do not know if these links can be strengthened to help people generate new ideas.

Many hands-on hobbies, like knitting, gardening, and coloring, have been linked to mental and emotional health benefits. Could this be the reason we're seeing adult coloring book sales surge? The benefits include better memory and attention, as well as fewer signs of anxiety and depression. The latter would seem to point to processes that would, formerly, be remediated with pharmacologic interventions. And it's not something complex that you need to do or to learn.

According to a study, handwriting is more connected than typing, which suggests that the two jobs use different mental processes. Higher brain connectivity has been noticed only when writing by hand and not when pressing keys on a keyboard. These results mean that writing by hand helps people learn. Strangely, greater connections between different brain parts are connected to the specific sensorimotor processes needed for handwriting.

In a culture that downplays students' learning cursive handwriting, we must question how this will ultimately fail them. This interplay of hands and mind is the "secret sauce" of learning and creating because it addresses the most relevant connections and is unexpectedly tied to our emotional lives. Writing with your hands is still the most basic way to communicate and paves the way for further academic achievement.

When we work with our hands, we engage more than the muscles. We concentrate on this because we know muscles are important in producing mood-changing hormones and directly affect our brains. But it's more than the muscles because we must also use our senses of vision, touch, and even smell when working in our garden, on an oil painting project, or anything involving hands and creativity.

It is an intricate interplay of all the forces we have at our disposal, and once they are combined, the effect is almost miraculous, if not still mysterious. Yes, it is mysterious because researchers have yet to discern the entire architecture of the brain and its many interconnections or those that may become involved in the future.

Think how much is still to be discovered when we consider the brain. It may be a couple of pounds seated within a bony container, but its mysteries are extraordinary, and no one realizes this more than psychiatrists and neurologists. Considering that we have yet to find the biochemical nature, in complete form, of any of the mental disorders, you have only one minor example of where we need to go in the future.

If we can use an increasing area of our brain and promote our abilities in any way, wouldn't it be in our best interest? We think of hand-related activities as merely utilitarian, but they play a much larger role in the overall scheme of our lives. Such activities enter our mood, sense of purpose, and whole being, both mentally and physically, and should be explored.

Unfortunately, too many people may feel that some of these activities are not worth their time, but what is life if not time well spent? Spending time in creative, hands-on activities is truly time worth spending. We may not need to go to experts to help us prolong our lives or improve our mood because that may lie in our own two hands.

Chapter 53: Gratitude May Be the Key to Longer, Happier Life

Recently, much evidence has emerged suggesting that gratitude is strongly linked to all aspects of well-being. Based on this, promising clinical interventions have been created, which fit with calls to investigate how disorders can be improved by promoting positive functioning and psychological strengths. And this isn't based only on studies that were short-term, but large ones that took years of follow-up and evaluation.

Looking at gratitude and death rates among 49,275 older women as part of the Nurses' Health Study Gratitude Questionnaire: In 2016, women (mean age: 79) filled out a six-item survey where they rated how much they agreed or disagreed with statements like "I have so much to be thankful for" and "If I had to list everything I felt grateful for, it would be a very long list."

Researchers followed up in 2019 to find out who had died in the study group. They looked at both all-cause mortality and specific causes, like heart disease, cancer, lung diseases, neurodegenerative diseases, infections, and injuries. According to the causes they looked at, cardiovascular disease was the most common cause of death among the 4,608 deaths they saw during the study time.

To get the most accurate estimate of how gratitude affects death, the researchers used a "conservative approach" that considered sociodemographic information, health history, and lifestyle factors such as optimism, social participation, religious involvement, and gratitude.

Being thankful seemed to protect against every type of death, but most especially against heart disease. Over the next four years, nurses who scored in the top third had a 9% lower risk of death from any cause than nurses who scored in the bottom third.

Skeptics might think that the study is skewed because nurses may be particular kinds of people who choose that profession and, therefore, are not representative of the universe of people who might experience gratitude. Not to worry; many other studies looked at other cultures and found similar results. Therefore, gratitude seems to have a strong, health-promoting effect on our bodies and lives. Naturally, it goes without saying that that also affects our lifespan.

<u>Getting Into a Gratitude Mindset</u>

Adding minor acts of thanks to your day is the best way to get into the habit of being thankful. One way to make your life more grateful is to:

1. Write it down: Write down something good that happened

either at night or in the morning. Set aside a notebook or journal just for gratitude so you can think about those times and remember them.

There's an additional plus to writing the good things in your life down on paper, which concerns cursive writing. We know that this can strengthen memories, and what better to do than keep our happy memories strong in our minds? So take a pen or pencil or whatever and write it all down at the end of the day. And don't forget that the good things in your life can be small ones, not major events. Getting up and being able to walk to the kitchen table can be seen as a good thing because not everybody can do that.

2. Pause: A lot of us say "thanks" all the time without thinking about it. When you say it to yourself, stop and think about what you are grateful for. Yes, you can thank yourself for some of the things that you do, and it's not bad if you say it out loud. Remember the very famous tennis star, Jimmy Connors? What was one thing he was famous for doing on the court? Right, he yelled to himself about something he did right or wrong and reminded himself what to do next. Remind yourself about the good things you do and what you need to do next.

3. Changing the way you think: During the day, you might feel upset or angry. When that happens, take a step back and look at the problem from a different angle. Sometimes, it takes a little stepping away from the issue before you can see it and then make any necessary changes. Not every solution comes immediately to mind, so give yourself a bit of time.

4. Send someone a quick note telling them why you are grateful for them, or have your family talk about something they are thankful for

every night at dinner. We don't need to wait for Thanksgiving to say what we're thankful for.

We should do this more often during the week and remind ourselves of all those things that we have allowed to slip by without giving them sufficient notice. Yes, there are plenty of things if you look for them. I'll never forget the Asian psychiatrist who told me about a saying in his country. "*What the mind does not know, the eye does not see.*" What is your eye not seeing?

When I taught undergraduate psychology courses, I always showed my students the film "Eye of the Beholder." In it, a specific circumstance is seen through the eyes of different people, each colored by their individual personality or need. It really hit the mark with the students, and they questioned how they perceived things, not just in class but also in their homes, where they worked, and in public. The film was always a big hit.

Start today; don't put it off, and help yourself see that your life really does have good things in it, but you have missed them because you weren't looking for them. Begin to look and remember, "Seek, and you shall find."

Chapter 54: Pain Can't Simply Be Rated As It Is Now

P ain can fracture a person's life in terms of their mental and physical well-being, just as an auto accident can change everything. Individuals in pain haven't received the care and attention they require because too many in healthcare adhere to the "medication-seeking" myth that is so common. If they provided adequate relief, wouldn't the patient become addicted, and if they became an addict, wouldn't they be seeking pain-relieving medications without genuine pain?

It happened in my family until we found an oncologist who understood what was needed. If you're at death's door, what does addiction mean? Relief is the only acceptable solution.

According to research, between 3% and 19% of people who got painkillers from a healthcare professional became addicted to them. It is not the rampant medication-seeking torrent of fake painkiller seekers the professionals thought existed.

It was a nasty, convoluted mental process, with lawsuits thrown into the mix because patients died. Some died after taking too much medication because their prescription didn't adequately relieve them or because their life circumstances had led to depression.

Either way, it was a lose-lose proposition, but pharmaceutical companies saw a shining light of profit if they promoted pain solutions, which added to the problems. Selling pain as a disease proved to garner billions in profits worldwide, and the infamous pain pill mills began sprouting up all over the country.

Anyone writing a prescription could make millions a year in income and leave their conscience in a desk drawer. After many years and many deaths, a settlement was reached with companies that were involved in selling opioids.

The realization that pain was not getting enough attention and was not being taken seriously dawned on healthcare professionals. People had long said, "Just take it, deal with it," even after surgery. Doctors were very careful with opioids.

A friend, after serious, painful spinal surgery, had an older physician (the pain specialist) cut her medication off and say she needed aspirin or some OTC medication. She needed more potent medication, and it took a nurse practitioner to see it. The older psychiatrist/neurologist was, as she said, "old school" of the "she'll become an addict" if treated. She didn't become an addict with treatment.

How Is Pain Rated?

The questionable pain rating commonly used spread like wildfire all over the country. That's because the American attitude toward pain changed in the early 2000s. From 0 to 10 was not new. Finding direct ways to check on patients' pain and talk about it with them was another area where nursing had made progress before the year 2000.

That being said, the 0 to 10 method became more common. After all, numbers can speak to everyone—not so much pain.

At first, there was a verbal scale with four levels: no pain, mild pain, moderate pain, and serious pain. One common analog scale had just one horizontal line that showed a range of pain or mood, with 0 (no pain) at one end and 10 (worst pain) at the other. The patient would make a mark on this to show where they fell. Is this reasonable?

Historically, the consideration of pain in medical education was abysmal. In 1983, researchers looked at 17 standard textbooks on surgery, medicine, and cancer. Out of the 22,000 pages in the books, only 54 pages discussed pain. Half of the books did not discuss pain at all. But one physician made an attempt at remedying the situation. Dr. Raymond Houde developed the Memorial Pain Assessment Card. He is known for creating many of the pain scores we use today. But pain rating remains elusive.

Nobel Prize winners in physiology or medicine in 2021 were scientists who figured out the mechanism for feeling cold and hot. But pain is a monster with many avenues that contribute to it. But a new assessment has been developed that may address this complex action.

The Department of Defense pain management task force developed the DVPRS, which combines several previously validated and familiar pain assessment tools with some important additions. The DVPRS (Defense and Veterans Pain Rating Scale) incorporates functional descriptions for each of the 0–10 pain levels so that successful pain management is also tied to improved function rather than simply getting pain to zero. The scale also includes an assessment of the patient-reported impact of pain on four specific quality-of-life indicators: activity, sleep, mood, and stress. This provides clinicians with a deeper understanding of the patient's pain condition and a better way to measure the progress and effectiveness of pain management treatments.

The question remains whether this new scale will be incorporated into healthcare as a general measure of pain in any patient. It would seem a new day for pain management may have arrived, but to ensure its dissemination, it needs to impress professionals in the field before it will become readily available. I've had one oncologist, who worked making disability determinations, tell me that he never learned how to evaluate pain in medical school, and there is no way to know what anyone's level of pain is. I believe he is correct and pain still is an unknown and an elusive symptom of illness or injury that has yet to adequately be addressed, even by this new scale.

Chapter 55: Suppressing Disturbing Thoughts May Actually Be Good for You

It may be a new day in how we think, what we think about, and what psychotherapists have been directing us to do all along—and it may not be what you've been thinking.

In the famous experiment done by experts in the mid-1980s, people were told to try not to think of a white bear. The people in the study were told to ring a bell every time they thought of a white bear for five minutes. They rang the bell more than once every minute. After that, when the same people were told to think of white bears, they did so more often than a control group that had been told to think of white bears from the start. Sounds like a curious experiment, doesn't it?

The results showed that *trying to block out negative thoughts led to repeat effects that made it harder to stay away from them.* In fact, trying to block out unwanted or negative thoughts is a way of reinforcing them. One has to wonder if there is a "cleansing effect" in therapeutic interventions that requires a person to discuss all of this material.

Many people saw the results as proof of Freud's idea that buried memories stay in the mind and can return to haunt us. It became common knowledge that suppressing thoughts is bad for you, and this idea impacted the field of psychotherapy.

And it is all wrong, according to some research exploring the benefit of inhibiting these thoughts actively. But then, much of what Freud proffered has been deemed as misguided and ill-informed hypotheses. The "god" did, after all, have feet of clay. There was no "research," just as there wasn't for Kubler-Ross' plan of stages of grief that she formulated while working with a few dying patients. What was Freud's actual contribution to research, and where did he begin to make money? Freud was a neurologist and he developed a dye for identifying nerve cells. The dye is still used today.

It is not enough to say that Freud's ideas changed the way people thought about studies and treatment. The effects they had on our culture are impossible to erase. These days, many people talk about ideas like the superego, transference, denial, and the unconscious iceberg.

Then, of course, there are anal-retentive and other little oddities he produced to support his hypothesis. Many of Freud's results may have been made up, as he would have ignored evidence when it did not fit with his intentions to support his own views. Whose dreams did he analyze to formulate that "theory?" His own.

This ability to forget, or lack of it, may change people in many ways. For example, if you cannot get rid of negative thoughts, you might find it easy to fall into a depressed mood. Not being able to forget does not cause sadness, but studies show that people who are depressed have trouble letting go of these thoughts.

Brain imaging studies are revealing portions of the brain that respond to various memory types, especially in persons with PTSD. One main sign of post-traumatic stress disorder is memories that keep coming back to you. Compared to memories of everyday events, intrusive memories have several traits that seem to go against each other. They, for instance, contain particular sensory and emotional details of the traumatic event and are susceptible to a variety of perceptually similar cues.

How Can We Do It?

To help them block out negative memories, some people might think about using **memory-swap techniques**.

Based on this method, people can change a negative memory by focusing on a distinct memory. Experts have said this method is like pulling on the brakes or steering to avoid danger. Here, we consider memory reconsolidation.

Memory reconsolidation is based on the idea that when we recall a memory, it becomes temporarily unstable and malleable. During this brief window of instability, it's possible to modify the memory before it's stored again (reconsolidated). This process offers a potential way to reduce the emotional impact of negative or traumatic memories.

Adding new relevant information (positive reinterpretation) after bringing up an old memory caused the positive reinterpretation to become part of the negative memory trace. This changed future memories in a beneficial way.

But people have different ability levels to control their thoughts, so this approach might not work for everyone. Any technique that requires effort to work against something, such as negative memories, takes time. As indicated, for some, it will be an effective means of handling these memories, and for others, it may not work as well. Is it worth the effort?

Undoubtedly, when we are disturbed by these types of memories that can affect our current lives, wouldn't we want to put some practice into this and see how it might work for us? If someone is working with a therapist, this might be something to explore.

As one of my professors said, everything in psychology is based on a sample of one. In effect, this means we are the laboratory and the experimenters. How it turns out depends on many factors, including our perspective, needs, and concerns. Of course, anxiety always enters into the equation, and we also consider that.

Once again, this technique will not work for everyone, and therapists may not wish to engage their clients in it because it doesn't fit into their therapeutic orientation or treatment plan. Some will say it's a bad idea; others may believe it's helpful. The advice here would be to keep an open mind because if something works, it's useful.

Chapter 56: Early Grief Has Powerful Effect on Lifespan and Biological Ageing

G rief is a part of life, not a disease or a disorder, yet too many will categorize it in one of those fashions. Grieving is normal, and there is no scientifically known way to stage it, but we are now looking at grief that reaches into the future. Losing someone, or even a pet, results in a sense of loss that can be unimaginably painful, but when it strikes children, there is a long-term price to be paid.

Worldwide, thousands of children are grieving after losing not simply their mother, their parents, or their extended families in war-torn nations. These children grieve a loss that extends beyond the family, including their way of life, their culture, their religion, the towns in which they lived, and the safety and comfort they expected. Their philosophical feet have been taken from them, and they are floating in a world of uncertainty. How can we expect it won't linger into their adulthood?

Children often lose a loved one, but their needs during this time are not fully known. While it is known that children and adults have very different ideas about death, not much study has been done on this from a child's point of view. The things that kids ask about something can tell you a lot about what they understand and what they need.

According to the results of a recent study, children who have lost a loved one may benefit from being able to talk about their feelings about death without fear of judgment. This could help them get the information and mental support they need.

<u>Facts Matter Regarding Death</u>

But how many adults still cling to the idea that children must be sheltered from the idea of death, loss, and grief? Many stories and schemes are concocted to not provide the truth of what has happened and thus permit the child to develop a sense of grief for themselves. How often do their questions go unanswered?

The things that children ask about death can tell us a lot about how they think about it. One important way to make sense of death is to ask questions and get answers. Caregivers say that children often ask, "Why do people die?" "Will I die?" and "Will you die?" This shows that they understand that death is inevitable and affects everyone. Often, the death of a pet may elicit some of these questions, and that can be a way to enter this delicate conversation.

I remember that, as a young child, when my father died suddenly, I was kept from much of the discussions and sent to stay at a neighbor's home until the day of the burial. The entire school attended the religious observation, and I stood with my class throughout, separated from my family. I recall wondering why I wasn't seated with my mother and siblings, but I didn't question it—that was the way it was.

Afterward, I was again taken to the neighbor's home and stayed there for several days. My family believed I should be cared for away from the grieving adults. The death was never spoken about from that day forward, and it was almost as though it hadn't happened, but he wasn't there any longer. No one ever sobbed in my presence, and I never thought to wonder about all the plates of food that our neighbors brought to our home.

<u>The Toll of Early Loss</u>

Many parents or spouses who have lost a child do not talk to them about their sadness to keep the child safe. Children may not show how they feel because they fear losing control or looking "different" from their friends. Adults think the children are doing well with the loss because of this front. Often, family, friends or spiritual counselors are asked to help the child or family.

Losing a parent or brother as a child is very upsetting. It has been linked to poor mental health, memory loss, higher cardiovascular and metabolic risk, and a higher risk of death later in life.

Researchers looked at DNA blood samples from people who had lost biological parents or parental figures, partners or wives, siblings, children, or parents during specific time periods while they were children, teenagers (aged 13–18), or adults (aged 18–43). Early loss as a child does carry over into later life with changes in biological aging.

They also examined DNA blood samples from biologically older people. Research shows a strong link between family loss and the health of children who survive it. The results show that faster biological aging may be a key link between being exposed to the death of family members and a higher risk of illness and death later in life.

Among US people aged 33 to 44, having experienced loss was always linked to being older biologically.

Grieving Behavior of Children

Children who have lost a loved one may show the following signs of grief:

1. After a loss, kids may be extra needy. They might not want to go to school or ask for help with things they already know how to do to get your attention.

2. Toddlers and children who are going backward in their development may start wetting the bed or stop sleeping through the night.

3. When older kids and teens have lost someone close to them, they often show their sadness by falling behind in schoolwork or failing classes.

4. Children who are sad may want to sleep with their parents or other people.

5. They cannot concentrate on one thing at a time and have trouble making choices or fixing issues.

6. They get worried about everything, but mostly about the deaths of people they know

7. The children may feel betrayed, ignored, or left behind.

8. Problems with behavior and changes in play with themes of death and rebirth appear.

The main approach is to communicate about the death in a way the child can best understand and, perhaps, seek a healthcare professional's guidance in how to best do this. In some cases, play therapy may be the best means of helping the child process their grief, and, as research shows, there will be a benefit later in life in terms of overall health.

Chapter 57: Awe Is Something Kids Need to Learn to Experience, So Teach Them and Learn, Too

A s a parent or caregiver, you can find room in your child's routine to incorporate wonder and its advantages. In our fast-paced modern lives, missing or passing up opportunities for wonder is easy. What a loss that can be if we fail here. And, while you're teaching kids, you benefit from wonder, too.

You might be more concerned with ensuring that a child moves on to the next event, competition, or tutor. However, when you learn more about the value of wonder experiences during development and understand what children need, you'll probably notice that children thrive when we prioritize awe experiences.

Some of life's situations can push us far beyond our comfort zones and the confines of our identity. This category includes awe-inspiring events, making us feel like we are witnessing something enormous beyond our present understanding. An illustration might be looking at the starry sky at night and realizing the vastness of the universe is not a canopy over us but something that appears to go on forever. We wonder how the universe can have no end. Is that even possible? Even helping a child to understand that the light they see from the stars is millions of miles away and that the source of the light may not even exist any longer—and this is awe.

Researchers have paid minimal attention to the perception of awe-inspiring experiences in early life. One study took a social cognitive developmental approach by methodically investigating how kids between the ages of 4 and 9 experience visually stunning acts of amazement in an effort to understand where our ability to feel awe first emerged.

Awe-inspiring events should stand out more and more in the middle years of childhood. During the years 4–7, self-awareness takes on more tangible, emotional forms. Perception of conceptual (rather than merely physical) vastness may be possible when the capacity for abstract thought and introspection grows. It is an important developmental step.

What Awe Provides to Kids

For children's knowledge development, the knowledge-enhancing function appears to be crucial. Inherently inquisitive and information-hungry, children are explorers. Because children's knowledge is always expanding, they will frequently encounter things that are both incredibly large in comparison to themselves and surpass their prior understanding—two essential components of wonder.

Around the ages of 8 and 10, kids start to develop more solid ideas about the world and themselves and feel more independent. During this time, the child's cultural self develops further, defined as their view of themselves concerning a broader group. Preteens and teenagers exhibit heightened social awareness, introspection, self-reflection, and extreme self-consciousness.

Awe can change how kids feel about themselves and how motivated they are to learn. Therefore, it is an opportunity to spark learning, inquisitiveness, and thinking ability in children and adults. Some researchers have separated the areas where awe would be inspired, and they include natural disasters, nature, slow-moving objects, and may include art, music, science (especially microscopy), and space.

How Can We Provide Awe Experiences?

Several areas for exploration for kids and adults alike can be easily found in things we may take for granted until we are directed to them. Consider:

1. The latest episode of the BBC's Planet Earth series and similar shows like The Blue Planet have many pictures like this.

2. You could look at the videos of Louie Schwartzberg. You may know him from his time-lapse work on the highly acclaimed 2019 film Fantastic Fungi.

3. Watch educational, artistic, or time-lapse movies that show the huge, mysterious space. In the NASA Image and Video Library, you can also find interesting sky pictures.

4. Collections of ocean photography, like the ones from National Geographic, can show you and your child how big and deep the seas on Earth seem to go on forever.

5. You can watch educational videos with your child that show amazing natural events, such as tsunamis, volcanoes, avalanches, and more. You can also think about how nature can strongly affect our society. How many of us realize that, at its core, Earth is a molten mass of lava?

The internet is a vast resource for these and many more awe-inspiring sites that will provide a wealth of new knowledge for children and adults alike. It is a means to easily inspire and motivate the wish to increase knowledge and motivate everyone to learn more and to experience it together.

One experience I had with several young relatives occurred in a movie theater. I took them to see a Disney film, and as the action began to use a Ken Burns effect to zero in, one kid exclaimed in wonder, "Are our seats moving?" For her, it was a new experience that sparked a wish to learn more and begin studying science.

Find the awe in your life and experience the joy of discovery and wonder.

Chapter 58: Do Pets Grieve the Loss of Their Pet Friends or Us?

S cience has always been either remiss or naïve when it comes to lower forms of life, or, should I say, non-human forms of life? We have always assumed human superiority in everything, especially emotions, attachments, and intelligence. In my humble opinion, this has been one of our major failings, but it is being revealed that there is more intelligence and emotion than that which is imbued in the human spirit. A scientific revolution in terms of emotion is developing at last.

The extraordinary documentary "My Octopus Teacher" showcases one of the most recent, albeit non-scientific, explorations of non-human life and, possibly, intelligence, emotion, or attachment. We knew that octopuses (or octopi, if you prefer) had an intelligence that permitted them to morph the coloring of their flesh to camouflage themselves when danger was near. But one thing we never gave a second thought to was that there could be an attachment, more than an interest, to human forms.

Perusing various sites on the Internet, especially Bluesky, we see instances of pets, dogs in particular, that have a strong, loving attachment to the people who "own" them. I use quotes with the word "own" because it reminds me of a man I met on a beach who was walking a large golden retriever. I asked him, "Is he yours? Do you own him?" The man looked at me bemused and said, "No, I do not 'own' him. He owns himself."

Emotions and Animals

A study of both dogs and their owners was subjected to a quantitative investigation of their reactions to bereavement. A total of 426 human adults who had experienced the loss of one canine companion while the other dog was still alive filled out the survey. This study investigated the possibility, nature, and severity of grief a dog may feel after losing a companion dog.

Researchers identified several factors, such as a history of food sharing between dogs, an owner's sadness or rage, and a friendly or maternal bond between the dogs, as major predictors of undesirable behavioral changes. When a companion dog dies, the remaining dog's behavior changes (in terms of "playing," "sleeping," and "eating") and emotions (fearfulness) reflect the quality of the bond between the two animals, according to the responses of dog owners. In contrast, the surviving dog's attitude was unaffected by the time the two dogs had spent together. Was this limited to dogs alone? Seemingly, it wasn't.

The purpose of another study was to identify factors that domestic cats are more likely to react negatively when a home pet dies. The survey inquired about the caregivers' and the remaining cat's connection to the deceased pet and any potential changes in behavior, both short-term and long-term, that may occur in the aftermath of the death of a household pet.

The more time the cats spent together, the less time spent eating, resting, and playing. In the aftermath of an animal's death, caregivers saw an increase in attention-seeking behavior proportional to the time the cat spent with the deceased. It was as though the cat wanted some emotional support in handling the loss of the other cat.

Cats, like dogs, undergo grief-like behavioral changes after the death of a companion animal; this was only the second documented study on domestic cats' reactions to this type of loss. But it's not only these types of pets that grieve, as was shown during a unique research trip near Greece.

<u>More Than Cats and Dogs</u>

While researching off the coast of Greece, an observer noticed a female bottlenose dolphin clearly distressed. Repeatedly, the dolphin used her beak and pectoral fins to propel a young calf—likely her own—against the stream and away from the boat of watchers. She seemed to try to prod her infant into action, but her efforts were fruitless. Unexpectedly, the infant had died.

Not only was she overly possessive of the calf, but her irregular eating habits put her health in danger, as dolphins have a very high metabolic rate. There were three more dolphins in the pod of around 150, but they did not interfere with the mother or do anything similar when they approached them. The dolphin mother was in mourning.

The subject of animal grief has now caught the attention of scientists worldwide, and anyone wishing to read more of an in-depth description of how and when animals grieve may wish to get a copy of "*How Animals Grieve. From fields to farms to homes and beyond,*" the author recounts tale after tale of animals grieving the loss of a buddy, partner, or companion.

Wild birds, too, change their behavior. When birds in a flock suffer the loss of a mate, they adjust by becoming more socially attached to the other birds in the flock and by strengthening the bonds between their own social networks.

The reactions of wild baboons to deceased babies were comparable to those of other primates: typically, the mother would hold the baby for a period ranging from less than an hour to ten days and would often brush the body, though there were significant individual variations, as seen in previous research.

Animal thanatology is now being recognized as a nascent area of animal intelligence, emotions, and group involvement, regardless of the species. The animals we love also experience affection and connection not simply to us but to other species, not just their own.

We've seen pairings of cats and dogs, different types of birds joining flocks that were not their own, and even young birds viewing humans as their mothers imprinting on those humans. Konrad Lorenz's unusual experiment showed the latter.

Chapter 59: No, You're Not Too Old to Learn Another Language

A great deal is written about ways to enhance or increase our longevity and how to thwart dementia, but not enough is devoted to learning a second, third, or even fourth language. Language is the key to so many aspects of our brain's life that we cannot ignore it or fail to nourish it with novel approaches to learning to maintain brain health in our later years.

One of the most potent means of improving brain health and increasing its ability to maintain flexibility, also called plasticity, is to provide it with new challenges, one of which is learning a new language. Of course, we could include computer languages in this, but in this article, I will stick to spoken languages.

It doesn't matter how many languages you speak presently; adding to your knowledge base regarding new language abilities is definitely to your advantage. Being an adult is no impediment to gaining a new language; it is an activity we should begin right now. And there are so many ways to do it, thanks to the Internet and language programs that are readily available online.

<u>Looking Inside the Brain</u>

Fifty-nine adults who spoke Arabic as their first language participated in a study about learning German as a second language. Magnetic resonance imaging (MRI) was used to see how the brain's structure changed as people learned a language. MRI scans were done at the learning phase's start, middle, and end.

Tractography was also used to see the nerve pathways in the brain on the MRI scans. As language learning continued, stronger connections grew between the language skill areas on both sides of the brain while the connections between the hemispheres weakened. This means that the left hemisphere, where most of the language centers are, loses some control over the right hemisphere because it needs to make more connections as you learn a language. A bit complex, surely.

The process was successful since learning German was hard enough to cause big changes in brain circuits. It indicates how the brain can rearrange its internal wiring to suit changing learning conditions—and it also means an adult keeps this ability. Children aren't the only ones who have this brain capacity.

<u>How Learning a New Language Affects Life</u>

Learning a new language can also help you stay mentally young as you age. A new study shows that adults who spoke more than one language showed the first signs of Alzheimer's and dementia later in life than adults who spoke only one language. The study looked into other factors, like a person's health, income, level of education, and gender, but the number of languages they spoke **was the most important**. Being bilingual for life is another thing that can help with brain reserve.

Scientists think learning a new language can help you concentrate and avoid being distracted. This happens when you switch between languages a lot. In addition, it changes how creative someone is. People who start to learn a language also learn about the society of the place where that language is spoken.

It helps you do more than one thing at once. Daily moving from one language to the other has been beneficial for the brain. As soon as the brain gets used to the hard work of switching between languages, it is easy to use this skill for other things as well. So, language is a means of improving many aspects of brain life.

Most people agree kids should start learning sports, music, or languages early to become good at them. This is because children who start learning late rarely become real winners or top musicians, and they rarely learn a second language as well as a native speaker. New results go against how true learning has been measured in the past, which indicated that people get better at many learning tasks until they are in their late twenties.

Another study sought to uncover further benefits of learning a second language as an older adult. These include brain health and overall satisfaction in life. It doesn't matter how well they learn it; the results indicate that seniors can experience improved health and well-being by learning a foreign language.

This means that the most important benefit for older adult foreign language learners is not how well they learn it, but how satisfied they are with their progress. This can be a good way to get people to improve their learning as long as they are in a safe and pleasant place to learn and are using the right methods to help them build on what they already know and talk about things that interest them. Specific language programs concentrate on the culture of the language, its history and using meaningful words and phrases that would be important to live in a country where that language is spoken.

So, foreign language teachers are very important to the education of seniors because their lessons and materials, when changed to fit the needs of older students, can help keep and maybe even improve their cognitive abilities and mental stimulation, which helps them age healthily.

A simple Internet search will find many free or inexpensive programs for learning a second language. Take advantage of what is offered and save more than your finances for later life. Several that are available include Duolingo, Babbel, Mango, and Busuu.

Chapter 60: Invisible Disabilities Need Our Understanding

Political conventions do little more than work to bring people together to elect a specific candidate. Still, in 2024, the Democratic National Convention provided an unexpected highlight: neurodivergent disorders. The individual running for the DNC's vice presidential slot, Tim Walz, has a son, Gus, who, standing in the stadium, exclaimed, "That's my dad!"

A young man with a neurodivergent disorder displayed emotion as he jumped up from his seat, tears running down his cheeks; it was nothing less than heart-wrenching. Those who understood cheered him on, and those who didn't took the opportunity to try to bring him down with cutting remarks and foolish comments on blogs and TV sound bites. They paid a price for all that, and one quickly deleted her distasteful blog post after receiving significant blowback.

Famed magazine editor Tina Brown and her husband, Harold Evans, have a son with one of these disorders. She wrote an article in the New York Times in which she revealed one of her son's actions after a party in an upscale area of Long Island. Brown's son, who lives with her at home, was at that time 38, and rather than seeing him as disabled, it has opened her eyes to his "secret power."

Brown's son's secret power, she said, was evident after a Hamptons party when he told the hostess, "Thank you very much. No one spoke to me, really, so it was a very boring evening. The food was OK. I doubt I will come again." How many of us would be brave enough to have said that after one of these upper-crust power parties? Undoubtedly, few, if any, would dare utter those comments.

I once had a neurodivergent patient in a large hospital where he had been for several years and where the staff on the unit believed he was a dangerous man, given to rages. His diagnoses were many, including intellectual deficits, anxiety disorders, and the inability to accept the fact that he was not white.

Being relatively new at the hospital, I was summoned to the unit when the nurse described a terrifying scene of someone "rampaging through the unit."

Yes, he was large but not very tall. His clothing was ill-fitting because they couldn't find anything to hold up his pants, and he had a rope instead of a belt. What started the alleged rage that day? The staff had gone into his shared room and thrown out all of his comic books and his precious Frankenstein videotape. He identified with Frankenstein because, even with his intellectual disability, he knew people related to him that way, and he wanted something that would have hope in it.

Once I talked to him, we began to understand each other, and he knew he could trust me. I began to accompany him to the ward dining room, where he had always collected his food tray, and immediately dumped it in the trash and asked to go back to the unit. Now, he would sit with me as I encouraged him to eat, and I would distract him with conversation. When I told him about famous Black basketball players, he became amazed and expressed his desire to have a poster for his room.

He had a severe case of social anxiety disorder that the staff chose to see as disruptive behavior and never explored the many facets of his personality. I managed, across a period of months, with the help of an intern, to reach the point where he could go to the dining room and eat with either my intern or me next to him.

Things progressed from there, and even though an experienced rehab woman said, "He'll never leave this hospital," indeed he did. He even went with a group to the mall. I can't tell you how ecstatic he was the first time he bought a pair of sneakers for himself.

The "monster" wasn't that at all, but a young man who was, in so many ways, terrified by the people around him and who tried to hide in his room as the only safe place he could find. The end of the story is truly heartening because they discharged him to a group home, where he actively engaged in all the activities, even accompanying the group to shop at the local supermarket.

We met there unexpectedly a few years later, and he yelled out to me. I felt an overwhelming sense of joy for him. His family was ecstatic that he had returned to the community and to the family that loved him. How many other patients like him are lingering in inappropriate settings and receiving too little attention?

Another patient I had at a similar hospital, who had been an abused, adopted child, had Klinefelter syndrome. Seven feet tall and with a love of making jokes and deceiving the staff with his little "lies" about hiding whiskey on grounds, he was a delight.

But the police on the grounds didn't see him that way, especially when three of them jumped him, and he broke an officer's arm. They immediately shackled him and took him off in a police car to send him to a forensic unit. He didn't belong there, and he didn't belong in that hospital either. I never knew what happened to him, but I did know that he had an extremely difficult childhood in the family where he had been adopted. In order to punish him for anything that they saw he did wrong, he was forced to kneel on rice until he could no longer kneel. It was cruel and I'm sure it affected him, but he always maintained a sense of joy whenever I saw him in the hospital No, I wasn't his therapist, but I admired his ability to find mirth in the most prosaic of things.

I sometimes wonder what happened to him and others like him who had been misdiagnosed and received the wrong treatments. He had great potential and I hope someone saw it and helped him to see it and to have a better life. Yes, therapists often think of those they will never see again, but for whom they hold special feelings of concern.

What Are Neurodivergent Disorders?

Primarily, we may associate neurodivergent disorders as autism, but it encompasses far more. Since the word was coined in 1943, researchers have been conducting an explosion of studies on autism. A developmental disorder now recognized as autism spectrum disorder (ASD) is defined by restricted and repetitive interests or behaviors as well as impaired social communication abilities.

More and more studies are shedding light on ASD, a complicated illness, providing information for all. Professionals and parents can benefit from a comprehensive awareness of autism spectrum disorder

(ASD) by reading up on topics, including the disorder's prevalence, its connections to hereditary factors, successful parent programs, and treatment options.

Some estimates put the prevalence of neurodiversity among adults at 8% worldwide. When people talk about neurodiversity, they usually mean a combination of conditions like dyslexia, attention deficit hyperactivity disorder (ADHD), and autism spectrum disorder (ASD).

It is problematic for employers because these diagnoses are on the rise among adults already working. When faced with neurodivergent personnel, business owners may ask how they can best help their staff without negatively affecting the company.

Should we say "on the rise in adults," or is it that the disorder is now being recognized as never before because it was an invisible disorder? Now, we are identifying more individuals with the disorders we previously failed to diagnose, and it's not just about recognition but also about being willing to assist them with their needs in society.

The Disorders Under This Umbrella Term

How many neurodiverse disorders exist, and can an individual have more than one? Without a doubt, mental health professionals can diagnose individuals with multiple mental health disorders, so it would seem reasonable that anyone with one of these disorders could also have more than one. The list is long, and some of the disorders are not often diagnosed.

Neurodivergent individuals may have some of the following symptoms:

Asperger's syndrome is now part of the autism spectrum.

Attention Deficit Hyperactivity (ADHD)

DiGeorge syndrome

Down syndrome

Dyscalculia is a problem with numbers

Dysgraphia, a disorder of writing

Dyslexia is a reading disability

Dyspraxia with motor control issues

Problems with cognition

Mental health issues such as bipolar disorder, OCD, and others

Prader-Willi syndrome

Difficulties with processing sensory information

Social anxiety

Syndrome of tremors

Williams syndrome (WS)

Additionally, researchers have recently discovered that eating disorders should be included in the listing of neurodivergent ones.

<u>Diagnosis, Treatment and Information</u>

The diagnosis is often made by a mental health professional, where an individual may have been referred by either a pediatrician or another medical professional who has noted special needs in this individual.

In neurodiversity, the emphasis is not on "dysfunctions" or "deficits," but on utilizing an individual's distinct strengths to compensate for their weaknesses and assist them in adjusting to their surroundings, be it at home, in the classroom, or on the job.

Individuals with neurodiversity may require individualized support to achieve their goals. Changes to the classroom setting, such as allowing students to use noise-canceling headphones, increasing opportunities for mobility, or granting students additional time to complete tests, may be necessary.

A neurodivergent test is a battery of questions designed to ascertain whether an individual's brain operates in a neurotypical fashion. Although the patient can do some of these tests at home, only a physician's examination can definitively identify a neurodivergent disorder.

Neurodivergent exams are mostly used for educational purposes. Seeking further information from a medical expert would be helpful for individuals who obtain high scores on neurodivergent tests.

There are many resources available online that will direct individuals to information on neurodivergent disorders, and they include:

Raising Children Net (Australia)

Children's Health Council

American Autism Center

ADDitude

ChildMind Institute

Association for Autism and Neurodiversity

Interagency Autism Coordinating Committee

CHADD

LD Resources Foundation

Autism Speaks

This is not an all-inclusive list; others may be found online. When searching, please keep in mind that some of the offerings may be privately owned facilities or practices, not nonprofit groups that provide information and direction for parents.

Chapter 61: Yes, Doing Nothing Is Good for Mental Health

It's natural to feel overburdened and constantly on the go in today's demanding world. We frequently place more importance on getting things done, multitasking, and being active than on pausing to unwind. But according to research, doing nothing—even something as straightforward as taking a break or a leisurely walk—can be really beneficial for our mental health.

While we're at it, let's put the idea of needing to take 10,000 steps a day to maintain our health to rest. Where did it come from, and is it true? No, there apparently is no scientific evidence to support this idea, which appears to have started as a marketing strategy by a

Japanese pedometer company in the 1960s. Got it? Feel better now about not getting in those 10K steps every day?

Now, let's talk about rights. We have one right that we are forgetting, and that's the right to do nothing at all, including those apocryphal 10K steps. The United Nations has a Universal Declaration of Human Rights that indicates that *"Everyone has the right to rest and leisure, including reasonable limitations of working hours and periodic holidays with pay."* If the UN thinks this should apply worldwide, why wouldn't we toss aside our guilt about rest and leisure (aka doing nothing at all)? If I said it was in your best interest for good health, would it be easier to do?

The act of "doing nothing," or things that require little mental effort, gives our brains a chance to rest and refuel. It permits us to become relaxed and let our brains roam, or what some call daydreaming, whether creative or not. What do we receive when we allow ourselves to do nothing and think for pleasure? Reduced stress levels and a general sense of peace can result from this.

But, according to one study, the problem is that there is an underappreciation of sitting and thinking that leads to a need to be actively engaged in doing something. The results suggest an inherent difficulty in accurately appreciating how engaging just thinking can be and could explain why people prefer keeping themselves busy rather than taking a moment for reflection and imagination in our daily lives. All of this reminds me of a piece of sculpture by Rodin, The Thinker. What must the artist have been trying to tell us, and how many of us got the message?

A well-known activity that is frequently linked to mental health is taking a leisurely stroll. Walking has many physical advantages, such as bettering cardiovascular health and enhancing stamina, but it also has advantages for our mental health and even creativity.

We may unplug from our devices and the relentless demands of our everyday lives by going for a walk. It offers us an opportunity to re-engage with nature, pay attention to our surroundings, and unwind. Walking can be contemplative because of its repetitive motion, which encourages mindfulness and lowers anxiety. It even has an effect on our weight-controlling genes.

Our creativity can grow when we do nothing. We give our minds room to expand with new thoughts and viewpoints when we allow ourselves to take a break from continual stimulation and distractions. Throughout history, many great thinkers and creators have emphasized the significance of solitude and downtime as sources of inspiration. Thomas Edison was a great believer in taking time outs and often took multiple naps during the day. What was the result? He had hundreds of patents to his name. One patent even indicated how the wildflower goldenrod could be used to make synthetic rubber for car tires.

It's crucial to understand that being inactive does not imply being ineffective or lazy. It involves purposefully blocking off time to rejuvenate. While active hobbies and regular exercise have their benefits, it's just as important to schedule time for stillness and relaxation.

Our mental health can be greatly improved by accepting the idea of doing nothing, even if it just involves taking a break or taking that leisurely walk. It boosts creativity, eases stress, and improves general well-being by allowing our minds to rest. A happier and more balanced way of living can result from incorporating these quiet periods into our regular lives. Try it and see what happens.

Chapter Sixty-Two

Chapter 62: No, Walking Backwards Is Not Strange, It Is Healthy

D o 25 million views on TikTok mean anything when that's the number of times people have watched videos on walking backwards? Maybe not if we dismiss this as a frivolous social media platform for wannabes, but when scientists look at the practice, it is a different matter.

Scientists know that walking backwards, or retroambulation, involves different muscle groups than usual and eases knee strain. Walking forward primarily engages the front thigh muscles, also known as the quadriceps or "quads." Conversely, these muscles are used to an even greater extent when walking backward. Ever see what team sports requires of players when getting. ready for games? They run backwards.

Increased quadriceps activity leads to a greater extension of the knee, reducing muscular tension and pain. Walking backward can relieve the inner side of the knee, which is a common site for arthritis in older persons.

Reversing your motion also engages the butt. By constantly contracting them, it strengthens your gluteal muscles. When you work out your glutes, you will also stretch out your hip flexors, which help your posture, balance, and spinal stability. If you suffer from back pain, as you become older, your muscles and joints lose some of their flexibility. The hip muscles are crucial for facilitating functional movement and easing discomfort.

<u>Why Walking?</u>

Walking is a vital means of mobility and has been the subject of more research than any other motor activity due to the strong correlation between it and health and well-being. An effective gait pattern improves movement efficiency and reduces fatigue. Issues in the locomotor system or neurological dysfunctions are typically associated with faulty gait patterns.

Implementing several simple things into our daily routine can reduce the incidence of specific painful issues and, possibly, even improve our well-being. We already know that exercise significantly affects our mental health and cognitive functioning, immune system efficiency, and mood.

When we look at something as simple as walking or walking backward, don't dismiss it as frivolous because it has a multitude of benefits, including:

1. Strength for essential muscle groups

2. Cardiopulmonary fitness and related health

3. Balance

4. Coordination

5. Reduction of pain in the back and knee

6. Increased mobility

7. Improved focus

Healthcare professionals are well aware of the importance of walking as a crucial component of rehabilitation for stroke patients. We know that those who have had strokes may not only have muscular disabilities but also increased anxiety about their mobility, and this causes heightened stress, which has a negative mental and physical effect in terms of hypertension. The latter can also leave a patient in danger of additional strokes. Therefore, reducing stress is of primary importance.

Exercise may have a milder effect on depressive and anxious symptoms in the general population than in clinical trials. Many theories try to explain the link between being physically active and mental health, but there are several things on which professionals agree. For healthcare professionals, extensive research has demonstrated that regular physical exercise can alleviate a number of mental health issues, including insomnia. A better quality of life and increased mood are also common outcomes of exercise. Plus, walking is something we do most days, so turn it into a great exercise routine.

I will always remember a man I interviewed for a book on muscular sclerosis (MS) who decided, after reading the research evidence, to start a program of daily exercise that included walking on a track. The results amazed him, and the improvements he realized were nothing less than stunning. Once he started his daily routine of walking on the running track, he then began to swim on alternate days and, to his surprise, his memory was improving, and he began to hold classes for seniors at his club.

How to Start Walking Backward

Going in reverse is just as acceptable as going forward, so long as people remember to be safe. Having a narrower view makes it more likely that you may collide with objects.

Treadmills are great for beginners since they allow you to hold on to the rails as you get the hang of the motion, and they also remove the need to look over your shoulder the whole time. Safety clips on treadmills allow users to deactivate the device in case of a slip, which is especially useful for older adults. Anyone with a history of musculoskeletal issues should talk to their doctor or hire a personal trainer before beginning this fitness program.

If you walk backward outside, it is best to stroll with a companion. As you move forward, this individual looks for potential hazards, such as other people or objects, or even traffic. Another piece of advice is to stick to well-known paths with few hazards. For instance, walking backward on an outside track is safer than a forest route.

Take it easy at first so your brain adjusts to walking backward. Professionals advise switching up for a half-hour stroll by walking ahead for two minutes and then backward for two minutes. Experiment with varied speeds and inclines as you gain confidence by walking backward or lengthening the time. Walking backward increases muscular activation because of the additional resistance.

Remember, start slow in a safe location and don't rush; go only as long or fast as you are comfortable. You don't need to quickly become a backward walking champ in your area. You only need to do it safely and reap the benefits. But also remember to consult with your PCP or a rehab specialist.

Chapter 63: Sleep May Not Be the Brain's Housekeeper, But It's Great, Anyway

S leep is something that all animal species do, which shows that it is important. One study seemed to show that sleep is very important for keeping a metabolic balance in the brain. Researchers used real-time tests to show that natural sleep or anesthesia is linked to a 60% rise in the internal spaces in the brain. They believed this led to a striking increase in the exchange of cerebrospinal fluid with other bodily fluids.

In turn, the research hypothesized that this sped up the removal of β-amyloid while you sleep. This particular material has been associated with the neurodegenerative disorder of Alzheimer's and may be involved in other neurologic dysfunctions as well. So, they assumed a healing effect of sleep might come from better removal of possibly neurotoxic waste products that build up in the brain and spinal cord.

Researchers indicated that during sleep, something incredible and spontaneous occurred in terms of the brain's size—it shrank. It was equated to a sponge being squeezed, and instead of water, neurotoxins would be pushed out of the tissue into enlarging channels in the brain that seemed to widen with the onset of sleep. Now, this too is being seen as requiring more intense research.

As noted, research over the past two decades indicates that sleep serves more than a restorative or memory-retaining function and clears the brain of metabolic debris that forms during the day. But now that research is being called into question, a mystery we thought was solved may still be out there waiting for a resolution.

Remember, not all research with non-human subjects can be extrapolated to humans. But much of the research to date has been with rodents or lower forms of animal life. Neuroimaging devices, however, will make future research more relevant since they will use humans in forthcoming experiments.

<u>What Are the Benefits of Sleep?</u>

Unquestionably, sleep is a vital necessity, and repeatedly, researchers have shown that either a lack of sleep or too much sleep can be deleterious to our physical and mental health. The science is in, and we know what to do, but do we do it? Or do we try to say that we can exist on little sleep?

Some research has indicated that lack of sleep or no sleep can lead to psychosis (as we saw in the Peter Tripp experiment and psychosis), mental disorders, and possibly death. There is a sleep disorder that is associated with death. It's called Fatal Familial Insomnia. However, it is rare and seems to be related to a genetic disorder.

We know that memory consolidation takes place as we sleep, possibly because there is a decrease in distraction, and the cells can do what they do to form memories. One thing that students have been told is to study immediately before they go to sleep to benefit from the enhanced memory processing that occurs during sleep.

Some people can function with less sleep, but they are in the extreme minority. Most of us require anywhere from 7 to 9 hours of sleep, and teens and babies require even more. Sleep can also be diagnostic when individuals indicate they need to sleep more during the day and night, indicating posssible impending dementia. In fact, longer sleep length may be a sign of early neurodegeneration, and as a result, it can identify people who are more likely to develop dementia within 10 years.

<u>New Findings on Brain Clearing</u>

Scientists believed that a major step had been taken to explain the brain-clearing processes that occur during sleep. The comfort they may have felt coming to this conclusion is now being questioned. So sleep isn't the brain's housekeeper, as we had been previously led to believe?

It is still not clear how chemicals and toxins leave the brain. There are disagreements about the physical pathways and how they eliminate material. It had been said that during non-rapid eye movement (NREM) sleep, solutes were actively cleared from the brain by the mass flow of fluid. This is now being called into question, even though we know a new brain-clearing pathway, the glymphatic system, has been discovered within the past few years.

New experiments show that brain clearance is lower during sleep and anesthesia, which contradicts previous studies. The authors of these latest experiments indicate that methodological errors were made in using dye to enter and leave portions of the brain during sleep. These errors, they believe, are responsible for the conclusions that were drawn and which are now being called into question. No matter what the process is, these researchers note previous conclusions that the idea that sleep's main job is to get rid of waste from the brain is debatable.

It is possible that the brain actively clears out waste materials as we sleep or even during the day. Until we have firm statistical evidence of the total organization and the many mechanisms of the brain, we will continue to search. In the meantime, this doesn't mean that you should skimp on sleep because it remains a vital part of our lives, and without it, there will be a price to pay.

Chapter 64: Laughing at or Demeaning Students Is No Way to Teach

P arents are our first teachers, and they lay the foundation for an important sense of self-confidence, self-esteem, and the ability to learn. These attitudes carry over when the child goes to school, but here is where reinforcement may occur in terms of loving to learn or believing that learning is impossible. In both these situations, teaching is of paramount importance, and it must be seen as such.

Students' lack of drive is caused in large part by teachers' discouraging attitudes and teaching methods. Relying on the same old methods that lack real-world associations is how you kill motivation in students.

Research has already shown that a teacher's mood has a big effect on how motivated their students are to learn. A positive and encouraging teacher has a positive effect on the behavior and mood of their students. Of course, another factor is how well the teacher is trained in the subject. They are teaching to students.

When I was a high school student, I had the fortune and the misfortune of having two different teachers over two different terms teach algebra. One teacher was terrific and knew the subject backwards. We quickly learned everything she had to give to us. The other teacher was required to step in when there was an opening and no teacher for that course was available. She did not understand the material well, and, as a result, we did poorly. It was an extremely disheartening experience for all of us.

One interesting aspect related to education, teachers, and students is David Bell's **disappointment theory.** Bell devised disappointment theory to explain how people decide what to do when they do not know what will happen and how they respond when things do not go as planned. Bell's work has been used in many areas, such as teaching and learning.

At its core, the theory has helped us study what motivates and interests students. Researchers have looked into how disappointment from unmet expectations can lower a student's motivation to learn and participate in school activities. This knowledge has been useful in developing ways to keep students interested in and dedicated to their studies, even when things go wrong. One thing we've learned is to make education a game-heavy exercise where kids eagerly chime in to answers that, under other circumstances, would be boring or anxiety-provoking, as in the case of math. In fact, *math anxiety is a major reason students fail or don't pursue additional education* that would prepare them for careers.

The idea is that an emotional attachment and caring on the part of an instructor help us understand how teachers and students interact with each other. Teachers have improved their communication and connections with students by understanding how disappointment can strain these relationships. Because of this, there are better ways to build trust and keep the lines of communication open, even when behavior or academic success falls short of expectations.

Even when results are imperfect, teachers now try to give constructive criticism that recognizes effort and promise. This helps students maintain their confidence and motivates them to continue to work hard.

One area where this is especially true is when someone is learning computer programming. Failing to produce a workable, always correct code is necessary to correct the errors and learn what needs to be done. This, therefore, points out that there are no failures, just increased needed information to provide success.

One patient I had quite some time ago told me that her father would repeatedly tell her, "You are so stupid!" As a result, she always felt a sense of inferiority, although she received promotions at her job and excelled at attending college in the evening. She never lost that feeling of fighting her inferiority, and she spoke with the high-pitched voice of a little girl.

I speak from experience, as I am a champion of teaching and teachers called to this noble profession. When I taught community college students in the evening, I always told my students that there was *no such thing as a stupid question.* I had mature students who had full-time jobs during the day and a family to take care of waiting for them at home in the evening. I also had students who came with physical impairments, and I can remember one woman coming up to me after class and telling me she was recovering from a stroke. She asked,

"Do you think I can do this subject?" I looked at her, and without a moment's hesitation, I told her she could because she wanted to, and at the end of the course, she got an A.

I encouraged everyone to ask questions so that they could fully understand what I was teaching. I also told them that if I couldn't explain it adequately, that could show that I did not have a thorough knowledge of that area and would have to explore it further. Therefore, I revealed my stance not only as a professor but also as a student. I did not present myself as the be-all and end-all of the subject area.

As I recall, in the first session or two, when we met, and a student would ask a basic question, other students would giggle or turn around and give the student an unpleasant look. I immediately addressed this and once again told the students that there were no stupid questions and that I would not accept the attitudes that were being shown at that moment. In my estimation, this helped the students feel more comfortable and see me as less of a threatening person. Not everyone comes to class prepared to be treated with kindness, emphasizing learning as possible for all.

I also told my students that when I was a student and found a subject difficult, I got at least four or five books on the subject and read how different authors presented the material. I told them that one author may not help you learn a subject, so you need several viewpoints to understand the material.

As a child, I also learned firsthand that some professionals have chosen to teach for the benefit of summer vacations and other perks and are intolerant of their young charges. When one of my sisters was in elementary school, a teacher's yardstick struck her, causing a lifelong injury to her neck. The teacher was aiming for a boy seated next to my sister, and she missed and hit my sister's neck. My parents did nothing because they believed teachers were gods.

I also sat in an elementary school classroom and saw a teacher smash a young boy's head into a slate blackboard. The blackboard cracked, and the principal demanded that the parents pay for its replacement. The teacher did not even receive a reprimand. It was, of course, a private school for poor kids.

Learning Perspectives

According to Alfred Adlerian's theory and practice, the best approach is to work with and help children grow and develop. According to Adler, "*A misbehaving child is a discouraged child.*" The best way to deal with bad behavior in kids is to help them feel valuable, important, and capable. But it's not only kids. It also includes adults who attempt to earn a degree later in life. How they behave and react is central to reaching their goal.

Alfred Adler's psychology examines how people try to compensate for how weak they think they are compared to others. These feelings of inferiority may come from instances where someone in their family or from teachers in school, especially if they were humiliated as children or had a certain physical condition or flaw.

But there's more here that needs to be included in learning. The results of a study supported earlier research and found that students are more engaged when they have good relationships with their teachers that are warm and encouraging. I had a university professor teaching a subject I feared, who made all of us feel encouraged.

He said, "*All of you are my students, and you will be my students for life, so if you need help with this subject, ask me. I am here for you.*" When he retired, it was a significant loss to any student who did not have the good fortune to have registered in his class. It was an amazing experience that I will always treasure. Unfortunately, after he retired, he died of Alzheimer's disease.

Consider the student who has special needs that are not apparent physically. This is particularly true when there may be a mental health issue (I have had students with a diagnosis of schizophrenia) with which the student is attempting to contend. A sensitive teacher, even without prior knowledge, can make a world of difference for this student, and that is where teacher influence comes into play.

Limitations or learning problems make it hard for students with special educational needs (SEN) to learn as quickly as peers of their own age. SEN kids make up 14.5% of all public school students in the US but only 13.0% of students in the UK. These students may not only require additional tutoring but also extended periods of time to take tests and even to remain in school before graduation. Some of them will be in school until they are 21, not the usual 18 we would expect.

<u>Teaching Goes Beyond the Classroom</u>

When I was attending college, not all universities were as open regarding testing extensions as we would like. One professor indicated that a blind student, who came with a guide dog and required special testing arrangements, would be one of the last students they would accept into his discipline. I can't imagine such action going without a lawsuit being filed by someone in the future. It was an incredible shock to all of us in the class.

Teaching may not be as attractive as it once was when women had few choices outside of remaining at home or becoming teachers. The pay has always been low, and the hours are long because lesson preparation is done in the evening at home, and student papers must be taken home, too. All of this, plus the inadequate funding given to schools, is disheartening and makes this career choice unattractive.

Anyone who goes into it today knows that they will have to use their own money to help buy some supplies for their students, such as paper, pencils, markers, sharpeners, and even printer supplies. This is where charitable organizations can provide funding for some of their projects. Other groups provide limited funds for student assistance in many areas of their educational efforts and social involvement.

For example, one group paid for a student to attend a special summer camp, another received funds to buy a simple dress for her high school graduation ceremony, and a third student received a suit to attend a family funeral. Not all of these may seem education-related, but they are surely in the service of self-esteem.

A student I had, on the doctoral level, took an internship on a Native American reservation. Enthusiastic and hopeful that he could make significant progress in student education, he soon found that he was contending with individuals who did not welcome him.

The library had no books, the science lab had one cracked beaker, and the children refused to believe that there was anything called an ocean. He pleaded with all his university professors and fellow students to send books and supplies and with major computer companies to send units. His disappointment was deep when he left after his six-month agreement. I know books were sent, but little else.

Ultimately, anyone who becomes a teacher must recognize the challenges and possess the qualities to support student educational development and help them realize some of the goals they set for their future. There will be days when they question their career choice, but it is truly one of the most significant lives anyone can lead.

Chapter Sixty-Five

About the Author

D r. Patricia A. Farrell is a published author of multiple self-help books and videos, a licensed psychologist, a former WebMD psychologist expert/consultant, a former medical consultant for Social Security Disability Determinations, a psychiatric researcher at Mt. Sinai Medical Center (NYC), and an educator who has taught on the college, graduate, and post-graduate levels, appeared on national TV shows, and on international, regional, and national syndicated radio shows, and in print media in national newspapers and magazines. She is also a top health writer for Medium.com publications.

Dr. Farrell is a consultant to pharmaceutical firms, writes continuing education modules for mental healthcare professionals, has contributed to USMLE medical school prep courses, and is a biographee in *Who's Who in the World, Who's Who in America,* and *Who's Who in American Women.*

A member of the American Psychological Association and the SAG-AFTRA union, Dr. Farrell is a former board member of the NJ Board of Psychological Examiners, a former psychiatry preceptor at UMDNJ, and a former board of directors' member of Bergen Pines Hospital.

Under a pseudonym (P.A.Farrell), she writes flash fiction that has been published over 40 times. Publications in which you can find P. A. Farrell's flash fiction include PicturaJournal, Jimsom Weed, Birmingham Arts Journal, Woodcrest Magazine, Literally Stories, Ravens Perch, Humans of the World, Active Muse, Free Spirit Publishing, Scarlet Leaf Review, 100 Word Project, Confetti, and LitBreak.

* 9 7 9 8 9 8 8 6 5 4 4 9 0 *